MASTERCLASS
in Italian Cooking

MASTERCLASS
in Italian
Cooking

MAXINE CLARK

PAVILION

Dedication

I dedicate this book to all my wonderful Italian friends from the past and present who have taught me so much about a cuisine that one can never know enough about, and that there are tastes still to be tasted and dishes still to be cooked.....MC

First published in Great Britain in 2002 by
PAVILION BOOKS LIMITED
64 Brewery Road
London N7 9NT

PAVILION

A member of the Chrysalis Group plc

Designed by Nigel Soper
Publishing Director: Vivien James
Senior Editor: Zoe Antoniou

Pictures on p2–23 courtesy of The Anthony Blake
Photo Library, except p14 by Gus Filgate.

A CIP catalogue record for this book is available from the British Library.

ISBN 1 86205 434 7

Colour reproduction at Colourpath in London
Printed and bound at Imago, Singapore

2 4 6 8 10 9 7 5 3 1

This book can be ordered direct from the publisher. Please contact the Marketing Department. But try your bookshop first.

All recipes suitable for vegetarians are marked with a [v]

Acknowledgements

I thank Sara Schwartz and Pia Scavia for believing in me in the first place and giving me my first opportunity to teach in Tuscany and Sicily. I thank all the Italian (and non-Italian) chefs I have worked with in the past for filling me with their passion and love of Italian food and cooking. Thanks also to the Ravidà family in Menfi, Sicily for sharing their house and their hearts with me, and to Stefano and Monica in Fattoria Montellucci for welcoming me to Tuscany again and again. Thanks too, to all my fellow staff past and present at Tasting Places for making it such an enjoyable company to work for, especially Annie, Natalie and Lizzie.

Gus Filgate, the supremely talented photographer and Penny Markham the magnificent stylist for this book, both shone with enthusiasm and talent whilst shooting, and together we made some beautiful pics. They are my friends and I can't thank them enough for their hard work and good humour – even though I hurt my back near the end and had to direct kitchen operations from the sofa! Gus's lovely assistant, Will, kept us topped up with coffee and cheeky remarks too! My thanks go to my wonderful assistants who worked so hard, rallied round and made my days in the studio kitchen such fun – Kate Habershon, Becca Hetherston, Christine Rodrigues and a visit from Julz Beresford! Finally my grateful thanks go to Vivien James at Pavilion for asking me to write this book in the first place and to my editor, Zoe Antoniou who had a tough time keeping me in line, but won through in the end!

contents

Introduction

I am passionate about the food and cooking of Italy. The more I learn about it, the more I realize there is to learn. However, as I have discovered in my travels, there really is no such thing as 'Italian' cooking! The country is made up of many regions, each fiercely different in geography, climate and the people who live there, and these variations are reflected in the local dishes and culinary traditions.

It is easy to fall in love with a country whose people feel strongly about what they eat and how they eat it. Conversations around the table are inevitably about food – how to prepare and cook it, where to buy it and the many stories surrounding it. I have been lucky enough to learn methods and techniques from several Italian chefs first hand, enabling me to teach Italian cooking *in situ* in Tuscany, Umbria and Sicily. Through these exciting courses, I have had the wonderful opportunity to meet and make friends with many Italians, and to appreciate their generosity in sharing their experiences with food and cooking. But of all the lessons I have learnt over the years, the most important is that the quality of the finished dish relies on the quality and freshness of the ingredients. They must be carefully chosen, smelled, squeezed and tasted before buying.

Cooking techniques in Italy are often very simple, but this straightforward approach, combined with the best ingredients, is at the heart of the taste, appearance and aromas of true Italian cuisine. Although the French may be loath to admit it, the origins of their 'haute cuisine' owe much to the expertise of the Italian chefs brought to the French court by Catherine de' Medici in the sixteenth century. With them, they also brought new vegetables, such as the artichoke and haricot bean.

Today, Italian cuisine has literally swept the world in popularity. It suits our modern lifestyle. Endlessly adaptable, we can use it to rustle up quick and appetizing meals when we want to. Or we can cook a special family feast that may require a whole day to prepare. There are no tricky sauces to master; what we must learn instead is how to cook with the heart!

In writing this book I have gathered together twenty-one exciting chefs, cooks and food writers from around the world, who are either Italian, have Italian origins or specialize in the food and cooking of Italy. All of these highly respected contributors have experience in teaching Italian cooking, be it of a particular region or more generally, and their recipes reflect their specialities. A dish from one of the selected contributors is highlighted in each chapter with special step-by-step instructions – a signature dish, a masterclass – giving valuable advice on how to achieve authentic results.

More than half the contributors for this book are based in the UK and have spread their knowledge of, and enthusiasm for, Italian cooking across the British Isles – and beyond. Anna del Conte is a world-renowned Italian food writer originally from Milan but now living in the UK, and is an authority on northern Italian food and cooking. Claudia Roden is also respected worldwide for her food writing. She has written an opus on Italian food, travelling the length and breadth of the country to research it. Claudia then made a television series of her travels, and has brought her deep understanding of Italian cuisine to this book. Valentina Harris, originally from Rome, is one of Britain's best-loved cookery writers and television personalities – in addition, she finds time to run a cookery school in Liguria.

Chefs and restaurateurs throughout the UK have also been persuaded to pass on their valuable tips and inspired recipes. Alastair Little owns two restaurants in London, both heavily influenced by Italian cooking, and runs cookery schools throughout Italy. His meat-cooking techniques are superlative. Alvaro Maccione, who I like to call 'Mr

Tuscany', serves traditional Tuscan food at La Famiglia restaurant in London, and his ebullient personality dominates his teaching! Claudio Pecorari is from Trieste but has cooked his way around the world, and was the creative force in Cibo, then L'Altro restaurants in London, where he banned spaghetti in favour of gnocchi! His gnocchi are now legendary, together with his knowledge of Italian cuisine... and his great sense of humour! Also vying for the 'greatest gnocchi' accolade is Francesco Zanchetta, the head chef of Riva in London, who shares his skills in Venetian cooking and the cooking of the Veneto, built up while working in the famous Harry's Bar in Venice. Giuseppe Sylvestri is from Capri and is the Italian executive chef for Harrods in London. His southern connections are revealed in his unusual pasta recipe from his native island.

Outside London, I have selected two outstanding Italian cooks. Mary Contini's family originates from the mountains of Abruzzi in southern Italy, but today they run the renowned delicatessen and restaurant, Valvona & Crolla, in Edinburgh, where Mary cooks and demonstrates. Franco Taruschio, meanwhile, left Le Marche and headed for Wales where he met his wife Anne. Together they built a restaurant of international repute, cooking Italian food with the best of fresh Welsh produce. Franco contributes his native Vincisgrassi recipe – a superb dish! Finally from the UK is Ursula Ferrigno, an enthusiastic teacher of, and writer on, Italian food, and a consultant to many food companies. Her knowledge of bread and vegetarian cooking is unsurpassed.

From Italy come five experts covering different regional cuisines. Starting in the north, Fulvia Sesani, who teaches Venetian cooking in Venice, has donated some rather unusual Renaissance recipes which are currently enjoying a revival. Moving south, Judy Witts Francini brings us Florentine delights from her busy cookery school in Florence, as well as her exceptional knowledge of ingredients and the history of Tuscan food. Carla Tomasi is a Roman with expert baking skills; her classes and effortless skills are a joy to experience. And, from her cooking school in Sicily, Anna Tasca Lanza shares her knowledge of that island's unique cuisine and lore.

The popularity of Italian cuisine, though, has spread far further than Europe (think of 'Ital-Cal', the phrase coined recently to cover the popular mix of Italian and Californian cooking) and to reflect this are recipes from both American and Australian devotees. From American, with a range of unusual and impressive dishes, is the world-renowned cook and Italian food writer Giuliano Bugialli. Francesca Romina is a second generation Sicilian-New Yorker, and she demonstrates her love of the cuisine from the old country at her Little Italy Cookery School. Viana La Place is a Sicilian-American who does wonderful things with vegetables, especially salads, while renowned chef Pino Luongo takes us through some favourite dishes from his native Tuscany.

Originally from Australia, Stephanie Alexander and Maggie Beer show us how to prepare some of the simple and delicious dishes that they teach at their cookery school in Tuscany. Their passion for the cooking of Italy, especially Tuscany, is palpable in the lively, colourful introductions to their recipes.

All of these chefs and writers have been selected for their expert knowledge of Italian food and their appreciation of the Italian way of life... and for their ability to communicate this to others. My own recipes which complement them are distilled from visits to *trattorie* and restaurants, through chatting and eating with Italians, and from eagerly reading my way through Italian cookery books, no matter how old they are. This new work, I hope, will inspire you to cook in the Italian '*maniera*' – with care, '*con gusto*' and with love.
MC

The regions and their wines

Abruzzi and Molise

This quiet rural area of high mountains and valleys stretches right down to the Adriatic coast, to the east of Rome. Due to the mountains rising directly from the coastline, there are few natural harbours and so the coast is difficult to access from both the interior and the sea. Fish dishes are plentiful around Pescara, including *brodetto* (fish soup), *scapece* (a sweet-and-sour fried fish dish) and fiery octopus and squid dishes cooked with tomatoes. Simple trout dishes appear in the mountains, and salt cod dishes can be found in mountain areas that cannot access fresh fish. Sheep, goats and cattle graze in the mountains and produce various cheeses such as pecorino (romano), ricotta and an egg-shaped cheese not unlike mozzarella with a crust, called *scamorza*. Cheese is very important to the cooking in the area and is added to many dishes. Lamb is highly prized and cooked in simple braises with vinegar, vegetables, wine and garlic, or threaded on skewers and grilled as *rosticini*. Pigs populate the oak-covered mountains, feeding on acorns, and are used to make Abruzzi ham and salami. Chickens and turkey are household staples. The forests and mountains provide game and herbs, as well as mushrooms.

Although blessed with all this produce, it is still a poor area and meat is eaten rarely – pasta and vegetables forming the staple diet. There are chickpeas, beans and some of the best lentils in Italy. Vines and olives grow, along with almonds. Even saffron grows on the Navelli plateau. Strong flavours are the order here – hot chilli peppers the most popular, along with wild thyme and poppyseeds – especially in fish soups made without tomatoes.

Durum wheat grown in this area and imported from Basilicata is made into good dried pasta. Fresh egg pasta is made at home for a treat and there are infinite varieties of pasta in this area, each served with its seasonal sauce. The famous *pizza rustica*

This market is in Orvieto where cooks can find the best and freshest ingredients that are vital to the Italian cuisine.

originates from here, the dough encasing three cheeses, ham, sausage and egg. Small cakes, pastries and sweet fritters take their place at festival times, and nougat is made with local almonds and honey.

The area doesn't boast great quality wine, but the quaffable red Montepulciano d'Abbruzo is a popular export. Native herbs and flavourings are used in digestifs such as Centerbe (100 herbs), *forte* and *dolce*, a nutty Nocino, an aniseed liqueur, Rosolio de Anice and a quince one, Liquore di Mele Cotogne.

Apulia

Puglia is the 'heel' of Italy, home of ancient olive groves and legacies of ancient Greek civilization. Bread and dried eggless pasta made from hard (durum) wheat are the staples and the cooking is very simple. It is no longer a very poor region due to the rise of wheat, olive oil and wine production. Old customs of hand-making pasta are dying out, but it is still made at home by women with time on their hands! Cooked pasta, *orecchiette* a favourite, is tossed with simple ingredients, usually vegetables or toasted breadcrumbs, to make a meal. Wheat is grown and ground into flour in mills throughout the area for the large pasta factories.

Almond trees bloom beside fig trees, prickly pears and fruits. Wonderful tomatoes are sun-dried, made into paste and dried (as they also do in Sicily to make *estratto*) as are chillies, and vegetables are preserved in olive oil. The vegetables grown here are typical of the south – aubergines (eggplant), peppers, artichokes, broad (fava) beans, fennel and asparagus. Wild herbs and wild fennel are gathered and used in many local dishes. Fish and seafood are simply prepared and served with a squeeze of lemon. Hams and salami are intense here in the south, and cheeses like mozzarella and *scamorza* are made daily.

Bread is a staple and *taralli* (little savoury biscuits) are eaten with drinks. Desserts and sweets are much the same throughout the south – usually very sweet and flavoured with candied fruits, nuts and alcohol.

Good quality wines pour out of *Puglia*, and some end up in the north to make vermouth. Wines from the Salento area are big and full-bodied – Copertino,

Fresh egg pasta in all its shapes and forms is displayed with different types of bread in this Bolognese shop.

and Salice Salentino. Other wines to look out for are San Severo, Castel del Monte and Torre Quarto. The Rivera rosés are dry and velvety pink. Rich *moscato* dessert wines are popular as aperitifs.

Basilicata

Next door to Apulia, this is the 'instep' of Italy, and almost the poorest part. It mainly consists of hills and mountains with a tiny bit of coastline and plains. It is very dry, but is incredibly beautiful. Basilicata thrives on pasta and the usual diet of legumes or peas, beans and chickpeas of *la cucina povera*. Many dishes are flavoured with chillies. Pork is the main meat, cured and made into blood sausage such as *sopressata*, fresh meaty sausages often preserved in olive oil, and the famous *luganega* sausage. The area also produces every type of vegetable imaginable, which are all carefully prepared. Lamb and goat are eaten for special occasions – usually slowly cooked to tenderize them. Fish and seafood are to be had in the coastal areas, highly seasoned with hot peppers or served cold with mint and lemon. Cheeses here are similar to all the others made in the south.

There is one really good DOC (a guarantee of authenticity) red wine called Aglianico. White wines of modest quality are also produced in this area. A digestif called Amaro Lucano is popular.

Calabria

The 'toe' of Italy, and its poorest region, has a very diverse landscape with food similar to that in Sicily. It too has seen Greeks, Romans, Arabs, Venetians, Spanish and Norman crusaders. Wine- and olive-growing traditions, dating back to the ancient Greek connection, are the mainstay of the region. Citrus trees grow well here as do chestnuts and almonds, dates and even bananas. Pasta takes the usual place, augmented by wonderful vegetables, hot chillies, olive oil, lemons and wild herbs. Honey and the famous Calabrian figs flavour desserts and fresh peaches, melons and nectarines abound. Inland, people tend to eat more lamb, goat and pork (in salami and sausages) whereas coastal dwellers have fresh seafood (sardines, anchovies and swordfish). Tuna and preserved tuna roe (*bottarga*) is king here, caught while on its way to spawn in the straits of Messina. Cheeses include *caciocavallo* and *provolone*.

Wine has been made here for centuries – in the land of the Sybarites of ancient times. Ciro white, red and rosé are good quality wines as is Melissa (white and red). The sweet, almost apricot-coloured Greco di Bianco (or Bianco di Gerace) is delicious.

Campania

Centred on Naples, this area is on the edge of the poorer south of Italy. Its cuisine is simple and heavily influenced by the ancient cultures that dominated this part of the world. Oil is king for cooking. Dried pasta – spaghetti, *maccheroni* and *vermicelli*, *orecchietti* and many other shapes, is cooked very 'al dente' and eaten twice a day. This is the home of pizza, the ultimate filler food for the poor appearing in all shapes and sizes, the Neapolitan pizza being thin and crisp.

An infinite variety of vegetables are grown here (tomatoes and peppers above all) and eaten stuffed, stewed, fried, grilled and dressed with olive oil. Little meat is eaten, but lamb is produced for festivals, and pigs are kept for the usual salami making. Fish, mainly anchovies and sardines, is simply prepared in coastal regions. Street snacks of stuffed dough or pastry are deep-fried in olive oil.

Cheeses are made from sheep or goat's milk, or, as in *mozzarella di bufala* – water-buffalo milk. Mozzarella is sometimes fashioned into long plaits called *treccie*. These can be eaten sliced with olive oil, breaded and deep-fried or served in little deep-fried *pizzette*. *Caciocavallo* is a stronger cheese, eaten at all three stages of ripeness – it can be fried or grilled. Fresh and hard salted ricotta, the product of the whey after making pecorino (romano), is used in sweet and savoury dishes. All these can be smoked.

Pastries are the favourite dessert here, stuffed with sweetened ricotta, almonds, candied fruit, raisins and pine nuts, and flavoured with orange flower water. Ice cream and fresh fruits are also popular.

Look out for lemon-flavoured sweet liqueurs served ice cold, such as Limoncello.

Emilia-Romagna

This is the true epicentre of Italian gastronomy. Bologna is its capital. Food is rich and complex. This is the land of the three 'Ps '– *pasta all'uovo* (egg pasta, in many shapes and forms, stuffed and unstuffed), *prosciutto di Parma* and Parmigiano Reggiano (now ubiquitous throughout Italy). Animal fats, butter, cream and goose fat add flavour to the rich dishes. The land is so fertile it produces soft wheat for pasta, tomatoes, and myriad fruit and vegetables. Cured pork products abound in salami and cured hams such as *coppa* and *pancetta*. Sausages like the famous *mortadella*, *cotechino* and stuffed pigs trotters (*zampone*) are classics from this area. Salami and cured hams served with figs or melon are a common antipasto. Usual meat dishes are *bollito misto* served with *mostarda di Cremona* (pickled fruit mustard) or game. Balsamic vinegar comes from Modena, as do *amaretti*. *Bigne* are deep-fried sweet fritter-like doughnuts, tossed in sugar. *Nocino*, a rich and sticky walnut liqueur, is a speciality.

Romagna is different in that the cuisine is based on peasant cooking, grilled meats, fish and poultry, anointed with liberal amounts of garlic and hot red chilli, unleavened breads (*piadina*) and plain flour and water pasta. Fish soups dominate.

Wines are made from the red Barbera or white Trebbiano grapes. Lambrusco is a famous one.

A fish stall displays the range of fresh catches of the day. The setting is Venice, a fascinating scene which combines the city's overwhelming architecture alongside the simple day-to-day existence of the locals.

Fresh pecorino (romano) cheese is being made here in Montalcino, Tuscany.

Friuli-Venezia Giulia

This area is centred around its beautiful capital, Udine, linking the three areas together. The former Yugoslavia, Hungary and Austria heavily influence this area. It is a mountainous land, but also has rather poor arable plains and some pastureland. It does not produce a great amount of food to export.

There is a supply of game from the mountains, and trout from the mountain streams. The beautiful, soft (and quite rare) cured ham from San Daniele is produced in the hills, along with many other pork products such as a sausage similar to *luganega*. Polenta is a staunch favourite, eaten with choice salami and grilled game, and the speciality here is a fine white polenta made from white maize. All the usual northern staples exist – potato *gnocchi*, bean and pulse soups, meat and game stews, risotto, cabbage and sauerkraut dishes as well as *gulasch* made with pork and paprika, and meat cooked with fruits. Goose liver and asparagus both have their seasons here. As it is close to the Adriatic, there is access to a vast range of fish and shellfish. *Liptauer*, the mix of cheeses, spices and condiments, originates from this area. Cakes and pastries include cherries, plums, berries, apples and raisins lifted with spices and honey and often stuffed with cottage cheese.

Wines from Friuli are only exported in small amounts, the most well known being Tocai Friulano and Tocai del Collio. Both are white wines, drunk when young, fresh and spicy. Other whites are similar to those in the Veneto – Riesling, Traminer, Sauvignon, Pinot Bianco and Pinot Grigio. Reds are from the Cabernet, Cabernet Franc, Pinot Noir and Merlot grapes. *Aquavitae* are made from pears, plums and peaches and many types of *grappa* exist.

Lazio

This essentially means Rome and its surrounding hills. Here again the cooking is simple, using olive oil, wine, pork fat, garlic and rosemary as essential flavourings. Pasta plays a great part, and this is the meeting-point of fresh egg pasta of the north and the dried pasta of the south, spaghetti and *linguine* being the most popular. *Gnocchi* are eaten here, made with semolina (durum) flour and cheese for a rich and substantial dish. Lamb, pork, offal, beans and pulses are frequently eaten in this part of Italy. Baby lamb is spit-roasted or simmered with wine and juniper gathered from the hillsides. Sheep's milk cheeses are eaten as antipasti with chunks of ham or salami. Fish, although plentiful, was considered to be the food of the rich and has no real tradition in Roman cooking. Artichokes and broad (fava) beans are great favourites, eaten raw or braised in wine and herbs.

Sambuca, the aniseed flavoured liqueur is taken after a meal as a digestif. The light, white Frascati wine, the Castelli Romani and the Colli Albani go well with Roman food.

Liguria

Think of Genoa and you have Liguria, a small region with a large port and a beautiful coast stretching back to high mountains. This too was briefly part of France, and similar local dishes can be seen in neighbouring Provence – most obviously *pesto* (*pistou* in Provençal). Liguria is a land of olive oil, herbs, fish and vegetables. Much of her trade was carried out by sea, especially during the Renaissance, so many ingredients arrived here, such as pecorino (romano) cheese from Sardinia and preserved anchovies from Spain or Sicily. Pasta is popular – *linguine* and *trenette* among the favourites.

The wines are light and fresh, like any coastal wines. White Cinque Terre is known best.

Lombardy

The powerful and famous Renaissance families of *Lombardia* greatly influenced the rest of Europe. Their land was rich and fertile, and they did much to encourage the cultivation of wheat (for bread and pasta), maize (for polenta) and rice (for risotto), along with the breeding of cattle, pigs and sheep for the table. As immense wealth existed side by side with extreme poverty so did two cuisines – the poor food of the peasantry and court food of the wealthy families. Traces of this remain in the regional dishes.

Geographically, this area is very diverse, and so is its cuisine. However, a unifying factor in the cooking is the generous use of butter and cream. As in Piedmont, these are products of cattle rearing, and some of Italy's most well-known cheeses come from Lombardy, for example, *grana padano* (a little like Parmesan), Taleggio, Gorgonzola, and mascarpone. Traditional meat dishes are stews and salami and preserved meats are typical antipasti.

Paddyfields cover the valleys of the river Po. The rice is all short grain, and numerous varieties are grown for different purposes, including *arborio* and *carnaroli* for risotto. Risotto here is served a little thicker than that of Venice.

Polenta (made from ground maize) really is the food of the poor; a staple to fill the workers in the icy waters of the paddy fields or ploughing the fields on cold mornings.

Finally the ubiquitous, but nevertheless delicious *panettone* is a treasure originating in Milan.

The Marches

Situated on the Adriatic coast, stretching from the mountains to the shore, *Le Marche* is a quiet and very rural area. Food production is mainly for the area itself. It is however one of Italy's largest producers of every type of truffle and wild mushroom. Pigs are kept not only to sniff them out, but also to make salami and hams, which are eaten cut into chunks. Cheeses include pecorino (romano) and *casciotta*, made from a blend of sheep's and cow's milk. Polenta is eaten with meat sauce. Pasta is made into rich dishes like *vincisgrassi* (a sort of lasagne). Vegetables such as tomatoes, cardoons, artichokes, peas

In autumn, squashes appear on vegetable stalls in many shapes and sizes. They make a wonderful colourful display.

and broad (fava) beans grow alongside fennel and large green olives, and forest fruits and berries grow in the woods. Being a coastal region, fish soups (*brodetto*) are popular. A flatbread called *piadina* is found in the north.

Verdicchio, one of Italy's most famous wines, comes from here. It is light and refreshing. Rosso Conero and Rosso Piceno are two very good reds from the area. Anisetta is an aniseed digestif.

Piedmont and Valle d'Aosta

Piemonte (meaning 'the foot of the mountain') is one of the best-known centres of gastronomy in Italy. This northern region, formerly part of the kingdom of Savoy, has many culinary traditions linked to France – a love of cakes, pastries and desserts, being one example. A region of high mountains, gentle hills and rich pastureland and plains, this is a centre of cattle and pig rearing, producing rich milk, cheeses like Fontina from the Valle d'Aosta in the north, and butter. Butter and animal or goose fats are used more in cooking than olive oil, which is not native to this area. Sausages and salami made from goose and pork are much prized.

The cooking is robust and hearty, and tends to be generous with antipasti and meat-orientated dishes. Classics include *fritto misto* (all sorts of deep fried meaty morsels served in a fabulous arrangement), *bollito misto* (fowl, meat and offal simmered together in a rich stock, a celebration dish to be shared by many), and rich stews such as beef braised in Barolo. Polenta is a favourite accompaniment. Perfumed white truffles from Alba pervade the markets in October, to scent game dishes or to shave over pasta and risotto, along with mountains of wild mushrooms. Desserts like *Monte Bianco* (named after the mountain, Mont Blanc), a confection of chestnuts and cream, *Gianduiotto* chocolates and ice cream made from chocolate and hazelnuts are rich.

Piemonte is rightly famed for some of Italy's greatest and oldest wines – Barolo, Barbaresco, Barbera, Dolcetto and those richer, sweet ones, such as Moscato d'Asti and sparkling Asti Spumante.

Sardinia

Sardegna is a land of shepherds and fishermen as well as farmers. They produce durum wheat and fruit. Their relationship with the sea that surrounds them is relatively recent, since they have lived in the mountainous centre to escape the malaria on the coast. Meat is popular – lamb, pork and salami, wild boar, hare and gamebirds. These are cooked on open fires, the flavour coming from the wood itself, often juniper or myrtle. Fish is now eaten and lobsters are a speciality. Mushrooms are found in the mountains while wild fennel and asparagus grow everywhere. Cheeses made from sheep's milk include *pecorino sardo*, ricotta, and one that is served to unsuspecting tourists and with maggots crawling in it! *Pane carasau* (or *carta di musica*) is the paper-thin crisp flat bread eaten on the island. As in Sicily, bread dough is made into beautiful decorative shapes for religious festivals. Sweet almond pastries are made from almonds and honey. *Seada* are ravioli pastries filled with sweetened cheese which are deep-fried.

The red Cannonau is a full-bodied wine for drinking with grilled meats and the Vermentino is a refreshing white wine ideal with seafood. There is a red dessert Cannonau and other desert wines (*vini liquorosi*) such as Moscato and Malvasia. Myrtle leaves are used as a flavouring, as in the liqueur Mirto.

Sicily

Sicilia has been invaded by so many outsiders that her cuisine reflects a little of all of them. There is a great Arab influence in the cooking of Palermo round to Trapani and Marsala – where the Arabs originally landed. Fish is cooked with raisins and pine nuts and desserts are flavoured with honey, almonds and orange blossom. Couscous is served with a fish stew and dried pasta dressed with sardines, broccoli, chilli, saffron and olive oil. Broad (fava) bean purée is served with bread dusted with sesame seeds. Tomatoes and aubergines (eggplants) are used in many dishes, topped with fresh or salted ricotta. Olives and olive oil are plentiful as are all citrus fruit. Salt is important to flavour and to preserve anchovies, capers and sun-dried tomatoes. Although now a simple cuisine, the rich employed cooks trained in France who created outrageously elaborate and rich dishes known as *cucina nobile*.

Food grown here has an intense flavour due to the heat of the sun and the volcanic soil. Game is found in the mountains, and fish fills the fantastic markets – sardines, prawns (shrimp), sea urchins, red mullet, sea bass, swordfish and tuna to name but a few. Cheeses are the same as in the rest of the south, but lots of sheep's milk ricotta is eaten. Desserts consist mainly of ice creams, granitas and sorbets, *cassata* and the famous sweetmeats made from marzipan.

Sicilian wine is light and fresh. It is made for drinking in its young state. However things are changing now as modern methods and new grape

This fresh vegetable stall is set in the Bolzano Piazza, in the Trentino region.

varieties are being planted alongside native varieties such as the Nero d'Avola. Good wine producers are Corvo, Regaleali and Donnafugata. However, Sicily's most famous wine must be the dessert wine, Marsala. It is made of native varietals. The characteristics range from dry through to rich and sweet, light to heavy. Florio and Marco de Bartoli are excellent producers. There are also moscatos from the island of Pantelleria made from the dried *zibbibo* grape, which are like nectar! As a complete contrast, a digestif or *amaro* called Averna is also made here.

Trentino-Alto Adige

This is really two regions; Italian-speaking Trentino and Alto Adige, or Sudtirol, which is German-speaking. Neighbouring Tyrol influences the cooking of both areas. This is a mountainous land, with alpine slopes covered by snow and skiers in the winter. The hills along the valley are lined with vines. There are forests where pigs are reared and wild mushrooms picked. There are even police who inspect your mushrooms for villains! Vast plains grow all types of grain for bread, including wheat, buckwheat and rye. Dumplings (*canederli*) of all shapes and sizes are popular in soups and stews, and *gnocchi* (particularly *strangolapreti*) of all types are a staple. Polenta is popular. Cream and cheese influence cakes and desserts. Cheeses made in this area include *Puzzone de Moena* (semi-hard cow's milk cheese), *Grana di Trentino*, and the hard-to-find ancient cheese called *Vezzana*. Cured and smoked pork is produced in the mountains and trout relishes their rivers.

Strudels, doughnuts and sweet dumplings filled with jams and fruits – especially apples – are another Austrian influence.

Trentino only produces one per cent of all the wines in Italy, but ten per cent of all the *grappa*! Wines here are German in character, from white grape varieties such as Traminer, Riesling, Muller Thurgau, to Pinot Grigio, several *moscatos* and *spumantes* from Giulio Ferrari. Fine reds exist with unfamiliar names – Fojenaghe, Marzemino and Teroldego Rotaliano. There are light red wines too, but they are not as interesting as the others. There is also a *vin santo*.

Grapes growing on the vine, with their vibrant and almost luminous colour, which is masked by a yeasty bloom!

Tuscany

The name *Toscana* derives from the region's ancient ancestors, the Etruscans. It has had a glorious past, especially when the peninsula was dominated by city-states. Florence was one of the wealthiest and most influential city-states in the land, both in trade and artistic achievement. Unlike in Lombardy however, Tuscan cuisine remained simple and rustic. Tuscans love natural flavours. Meats plainly grilled on an open wood fire, especially Chianina and Maremmana beef, and poultry are still preferred, with spatchcocking or flattening a popular technique. Cooking with wine, sage, rosemary and basil enhances the flavour.

The countryside is diverse with woods, hills and coast, so game (wild boar, hare and pheasant) and wild mushrooms are greatly prized. Game is also stewed or made into rich sauces for pasta (*pappardelle alla lepre*, pasta ribbons with hare sauce). Tripe is a great favourite. Olives for oil and vines for wine were grown together. Olives and grapes are the main crops. Tuscan olive oils, many with a slightly peppery after-taste, are some of the best in Italy, although production is small. Pecorino (romano) sheep's milk cheese, ranges from soft and fresh to mature for grating and makes a favourite antipasto dish with raw, fresh young broad (fava) beans. Chestnuts are ground into flour and made into a polenta-type porridge or a flat cake which is called *castagnaccio*. Bread and salt play an important part in this hearty cuisine. The Tuscans have earned the nickname of *mangiafagioli* – the bean-eaters, and they do love beans, both fresh and dried, in soups (*ribollita*, *zuppa di fagioli*), salads and in pasta dishes. Meals are ended simply with fruit or *cantuccini* (biscuits) to dip in *vin santo*. There are few desserts but some local specialities include *ricciarelli* (soft almond biscuits) and the nutty fruit and spice concoction *panforte*, both from Siena.

Tuscany produces great wines such as Chianti, Chianti Classico, Brunello, the Barolo from Piedmont, the Brunello de Montalcino, Vino Nobile de Montepulciano, whites such as Vernaccia di San Gimignano, and the sweet wine *vin santo*.

Umbria

This beautiful land-locked area of Italy lies next to Tuscany, and has a similar simple cuisine. Cooking takes note of the seasons, particularly in the autumn when dishes feature wild mushroom and game. Norcia is the centre of gastronomy, renowned for black and white truffles from the surrounding area, adding sophistication to many dishes here. Pork products such as sausages, salami and hams abound, and are quite strong in flavour. As in Tuscany *porchetta* is sold in all the street markets – this is a whole pig, slow roasted in a wood oven overnight, with slices

Another fruit and vegetable store, revealing the produce of the Emilia-Romagna region, displays asparagus, grapes, peaches and other fruit.

stuffed into bread with crackling. Sheep produce cheese and are sold as lamb for the barbecue, as are freshwater fish such as trout. Lentils from Castelluccio are considered to be the best in Italy and the well-known Buitoni pasta is made here. Umbrian olive oil is light and perfumed and is used in all cooking. Meals end with fruit or *biscotti*.

Orvieto and Torgiano are crisp and dry whites, although Tuscany is the leader. The red Torgiano Riserva is excellent. *Vin santo* is also produced here.

Veneto

Having been the one of the most important trading cities in the known world during the Renaissance, Venice and its surrounding area adopted many styles of cooking and ingredients from all who visited – in particular the Arabs. The trade with the east introduced a simple sweet-sour flavour combination using vinegar, currants and raisins, pine nuts and sometimes capers. Salt cod or stockfish is still a favourite.

Most of the cooking of the area is simple and revolves around the fish and seafood from the sea, lagoon and lakes, although pork products (*cotechino* and *luganega*), salami and cured meats play their part. Calves' liver is eaten conspicuously in Venice more than anywhere else in this region. Risotto is also popular, here given a more soupy, creamy consistency than elsewhere, and it is flavoured in many ways, from game to squid ink. Polenta appears in a soft, almost mashed-potato form, and there are plenty of beans and bean soups. White asparagus is revered in the spring, to be cooked simply and served with melted butter and hard-boiled eggs. Vegetables abound, the most famous being radicchio and particularly the *radicchio di Treviso* with its long, bitter leaves of purple-pink. Tiny game birds, all types of poultry and wild duck, and game from the marshes and lagoons are eaten with relish! Venetians also prize their salt, gleaned from the salt marshes.

The famous *pandoro* (a little like panettone) is baked at Christmas, and *tiramisù* is thought to have originated here. There is also *biscotti* and ice cream.

Wines include Bardolino, Valpolicella, Amarone, Pinot Grigio, and the sparkling Prosecco, some of the best in Italy. *Grappa* also makes its mark here.

The Italian store cupboard

Anchovies (*Acciughe, alici*)

Whether salted or in oil, these are essential to give a piquant savouriness to some Italian dishes, especially those from the south. They have been a firm favourite since Roman times. Salted anchovies (*acciughe sotto sale*) are the whole fish (mostly without head) preserved in salt, and need to be rinsed, split open and their backbone extracted. They come in jars or larger tins. Salted anchovies have a fresher taste than those preserved in oil (*filetti di acciuga*). They also look better, as they retain their silvery skin. Both can be soaked in milk or water to soften them and remove excess salt. Anchovy paste is a good standby to have in your larder.

Bottarga (*Uova di tonno*)

This is tricky to find even in Italy. It is the salted, pressed and dried roe of the tuna or grey mullet and can be an acquired taste – you love it or hate it. It tastes of concentrated fish and is used sparingly to dress pasta (grated) or when very fresh, thinly sliced and served with a squeeze of lemon. It is found in southern Italy and Sicily and the mullet is found in Sardinia. It is sold by weight in a piece or ready cut and vacuum packed. It is also found in small jars, dried and finely grated like Parmesan, to mix into pasta with chilli, garlic and parsley. Always bring some back when visiting Italy – it freezes well.

Breadcumbs (*Pangrattato*)

There is no waste in an Italian household and bread is no exception. Leftover bread is dried and made into breadcrumbs – an essential part of Italian cuisine everywhere. Store in an airtight container.

Capers (*Capperi*)

These are the flower buds of a leathery-leaved Mediterranean plant, which readily grows in the poorest of soils in the wild. The buds are carefully

Trays of freshly prepared anchovies are displayed in a fish market at Elba Portoferráio in Tuscany.

hand-picked, dried and preserved layered in coarse salt or in vinegar. Both types should be well-rinsed before using, and can be soaked in cold water for a while to soften the flavour. Caper berries are the seed pod of the bush, if the flowers are left to fruit. They are preserved in the same way and are often served as a garnish or with cold meats and cheeses. The best capers are said to be the smallest and come from the islands of Pantelleria and Salina, which are off Sicily.

Cheese (*Formaggio*)

Caciocavallo, a Sicilian cheese made from cow's milk, is the 'cheddar' of the country. It is a semi-hard cooked cheese with a plastic texture. It comes in rectangular blocks. *Provolone* is a good substitute.

Caciotta from Campania and Lazio is made from cow's, ewe's or goat's milk and is a small flat disc with a washed rind rather like pecorino (romano). It is a country cheese.

Canestrato is a hard Sicilian cheese similar to aged *pecorino romano* made from cow's and goat's milk. The curds are pressed into round rush baskets (*canestrati*), then turned out and cooked again. It has a hard rind, rubbed with salt and can be flavoured with black pepper or chilli. It is nutty and piquant.

Fontina is a mountain cheese and comes from the Valle d'Aosta. The cheese is made in huge wheels, has a washed rind and is matured in caves and grottoes for at least three months. The cheese has a soft buttery taste and melts beautifully.

Gorgonzola is a rich cow's milk cheese from Lombardy. *Dolce* is mild and *piccante* is strong.

Mascarpone is a fresh thick cheese made from cream (like cream cheese, but with a richer flavour and smoother texture), and is used for desserts.

Mozzarella is traditionally made from water buffalo milk (*mozzarella di bufala*), but is made with cow's milk too. It is snowy white when fresh and springy. It is usually sold sitting in its own whey to keep it moist. Tiny *mozzarelle* are called *bocconcini*.

Parmigiano (Parmesan) is a hard *grana* cheese. It is salty and crumbly and has a pale straw colour.

Parmigiano reggiano is the best, but *grana padano* is cheaper and just as good in cooking. Shaving Parmesan onto salads is a current fashion while it is normally finely ground. It is used liberally in northern cuisine, especially in risottos. It is never used on or with seafood.

Pecorino (romano) – all *pecorino* is made from ewe's milk (*latte di pecora*) and comes from central and southern Italy. It is a washed rind semi-hard cheese and there are many regional varieties. *Pecorino toscano* (sometimes known as *canestrato* and *marzolino*) is ripe within two weeks and has a soft creamy centre with a delicate flavour. The longer it matures the sharper and stronger the flavour.

Pecorino sardo and pecorino romano both come from Sardinia (some from Lazio). They are robust in flavour and are ready for the table after five months maturing, and at eight months they are ready for grating. They become firmer and drier with time, and have a tangy flavour. *Pecorino romano* is cooked twice before maturing. Some *pecorini* are smoked.

Pecorino siciliano is made from raw ewe's milk (*latte di pecora*). The new fresh cheese is 'tuma' and is very elastic. After two weeks ageing it becomes 'primo sale' (waxy) and after four months it can be grated. It sometimes has black peppercorns added. The cheese has an ivory white rind with the marks of the rush basket and the inside is creamy white, becoming harder as it matures.

Provolone is a waxy curd cheese originally made from cow and water buffalo milk in Campania and Apulia, but is also made in Lombardy. It is kneaded into rounds, ovals, pear shapes or huge tubes, and can vary in size. The mature cheese is *piccante* (piquant), and the young cheese is *dolce* (sweet). It is sometimes smoked.

Ricotta is a soft cheese made from leftover whey (from the daily cheese production) which is reheated and the little coagulated lumps of curd are strained off and transferred to a rush basket to drain for three to four hours. It is ready to eat at this stage. It should be snowy-white and sweet – it is also sold in a harder salted version, which is good in salads. It can be made from cow's or sheep's (*ricotta di pecora*) milk. *Ricotta di pecora* is extensively used in Sicily and the south. In parts of Sicily there is a type of ricotta that is coated in salt and smoked in a wood-fired oven.

Huge pieces of Parmesan cheese are stacked high for selling at a market stall. These are cut into pieces and weighed. Locally made salami hangs in the background.

Chillies (*Peperoncini*)

Both dried and fresh chillies are used in abundance, especially in the south and in Tuscany. Italians use chilli flakes when fresh is not available. The heat of the chilli depends on the season and the variety – remove the seeds for less heat, and use rubber gloves or wash your hands immediately and don't touch your eyes, if you don't want to be burnt.

Flour (*Farina*)

There are two main types of flour used throughout Italy. *Farina di grano tenero* – the finest, whitest grade of soft wheat flour (*Triticum aestivum*) and *semolino di grano duro* or hard wheat semolina flour (*Triticum durum*), which is made from the hard heart of the wheat so has a higher gluten content. This is the flour used for making commercial dried pasta, southern eggless pasta, Sicilian breads and pizza. Hard wheat flour gives pasta a firmer texture and is better than ordinary flour for dusting fresh pasta to prevent sticking – it is coarser and so falls off the pasta during cooking. Chickpea flour (*farina di ceci*) is mainly used in the south and Sicily to make *panelle* – chickpea fritters, sold as street food. A type of chickpea flat bread (*farinata*) is made in Liguria. '00' and '0' means the grade of the flour, double zero being the finest.

Flower water (*Estratto dei fiori*)

Orange flower water, rosewater and jasmine water were brought to Sicily by the Arabs, and are used to delicately perfume in sweets, pastries, salads and desserts. They are especially good with almonds.

Dried and candied fruit (*Uva passa e frutta candita*)

Uva passa are raisins, and golden *sultanina* raisins are found in Sicily along with the truly amazing almost enormous, muscat-like *zibbibo* raisins from Pantelleria. Currant-like *uvetta* are used in desserts and savoury dishes alike. Candied fruit (*frutta candita*) and peel is used with abandon in desserts and baking – this was brought by returning crusaders to mainland Italy, and by the conquering Arabs to Sicily. The further south, the sweeter the tooth!

Garlic (*Aglio*)

Garlic is used in many ways to give a vast range of flavours. The larger the cloves (and heads) of garlic, the sweeter it will be, especially if still purply-green and fresh. Small hard heads of garlic tend to be bitter and strong. The softer and fresher the garlic, the more subtle the flavour. When frying garlic, do not let it colour too much or it can go bitter.

Ham (*Prosciutto*)

Prosciutto is the generic term for ham. *Prosciutto crudo* is raw cured ham, and *prosciutto di Parma* is a particularly high quality *prosciutto crudo*. *Prosciutto* is made from the hind leg (thigh) of well-fed pigs, which is trimmed of excess fat, cleaned and buried in salt for up to twenty-five days depending on the type or custom. The ham is then brushed clear of salt and hung in a cool dry place for a month to rest before being aged and dressed with a coating of fat, salt and flour. Only three types of *prosciutti* have the DOC mark (*Denominazione di Origine Controllata* – a guarantee of origin): Parma, San Daniele and Veneto. *Prosciutto di Parma* is made from pigs fed on the whey left over from making Parmesan and is considered the finest and best. It is quite pale. San Daniele has a redder colour and is stronger in flavour.

Strings or treccie *of fresh garlic, or* aglio, *hang ready for picking with their soft pink skins.*

Fresh San Daniele hams (below) are waiting to be distributed to sellers and shops.

Prosciutto Veneto is delicate and sweet. There are many different types of *prosciutto crudo* in central Italy and no Italian refrigerator would be without it to keep at hand. If you just ask for *prosciutto* in Italy, they will ask '*crudo o cotto?*' – raw or cooked.

Herbs (*Erbe*)

Basil (*basilico*) is mainly used raw and is never cut, but torn to save the volatile oils. It is strewn over salads and is the main ingredient in *pesto alla Genovese* (pesto sauce).

Bay leaves (*alloro*) are used to flavour soups, sauces and stews and are particular to Sicilian food.

Mint (*menta*) is used extensively in Sicily and the south – a legacy from the Arab domination, it is used in both sweet and savoury dishes.

Nepitella is a type of wild catmint used with mushroom dishes, especially in Tuscany and Sicily.

Oregano (*oregano*), a wild form of marjoram, is generally best used dried. It has a better flavour this way – you see it hanging in bunches in markets during the season, then crumbled into bags when the season is over. Crumble it between your fingers to release the aroma.

Parsley (*prezzemolo*) is used in everything, but is usually the continental flat-leaf type.

Rosemary (*rosmarino*) is used widely in meat and game dishes – especially in the mountainous north and central Italy. It is better used fresh than dried.

Sage (*salvia*) is used in stuffings and to flavour meats and game. The leaves are very strong in flavour and are used sparingly. A popular pre-drink nibble is deep-fried sage leaves.

Tarragon (*dragoncello*) is used with chicken and fish and some tomato dishes.

Dried thyme (*timo*) is good too especially in meat and game dishes.

Mushrooms (*Funghi*)

Dried wild mushrooms (*funghi porcini secchi*): the most famous and prized wild mushroom is the *porcino* (*Boletus edulis*). It is gathered during the autumn months and much coveted. Dried mushrooms come in different grades – slices, pieces and little pieces, which are priced accordingly. They

should be eaten within a year of drying and should be kept in an airtight jar. They need to be soaked in tepid water for twenty minutes before using – keep the soaking water; it will add loads of flavour to a sauce, soup or stew.

Wild mushrooms (*funghi*): in August and September all Italy takes to their patch of woodland early in the morning, to search for wild mushrooms – *porcini* (ceps) and *gallinaci* (*chanterelles* or *girolles*) being the most popular. Armed with sticks and baskets, people disappear to their secret places two to three days after rain to see what has popped up under the leaves. It is the combination of warmth from the sun and dampness from the rain that coaxes them out of the ground, but they must be picked before the slugs and flies get to them. There are simply not enough wild mushrooms to satisfy the voracious Italian appetite, and mushrooms are imported from eastern Europe. They are added to polenta, pies, risottos and stews. Brushed with olive oil, whole mushrooms are grilled over wood fires with garlic. Some are simply pan-fried with olive oil and garlic, then strewn with parsley. Sauces are made for pasta and some dried pasta is even flavoured with wild mushroom. Italians love to dry and freeze wild mushrooms for later. Some mushrooms are preserved

Porcini and other freshly picked mushrooms, fruits and vegetables are beautifully presented on a stall in Bologna.

in oil. *Ovoli* are mushrooms that look like eggs with a yellow yolk, are highly prized and are served raw in thin slices. Mushrooms must be carefully cleaned by brushing and are never washed.

Nuts (*Noce*)

Chestnuts (*castagne*) are roasted fresh to munch with new red wine, dried for soups and stews, candied for desserts and even made into a flour to make *castagnaccio*, a sweet chestnut and rosemary cake from Tuscany.

Hazelnuts (*nocciole*), walnuts (*noce*) and almonds (*mandorle*) are used extensively in desserts and sweets as well as to thicken sauces and some soups.

Pine kernels (*pinoli*), the seeds of pine cones from the stone pine, are expensive, as their extraction is labour-intensive. They are generally not toasted.

Olive oil (*Olio d'oliva or uliva*)

Olive oil is essential to Italian cuisine, and the choice is limitless – some are peppery, some grassy and some have a hint of almond. There are six grades of cold-pressed olive oil, the finest being *olio d'oliva extra vergine*, extra virgin olive oil (up to one per cent acidity) for dressing salads and drizzling over meat or soups, and the quality is expressed in the price. Use a lighter less expensive oil like *olio d'oliva vergine* (up to three and a half per cent acidity) for cooking and baking. A dark green olive oil does not necessarily guarantee quality; it depends on the type of olive used – taste it and see. Buy the best olive oil you can afford for drizzling and dressing and a cheaper supermarket one for frying. Don't keep the oil in direct light or in a hot place – the refrigerator or cool larder is best. It may solidify, but leave it out in the room for a couple of minutes to loosen up. It should be consumed within a year of pressing – it can go rancid. Contrary to popular belief, olive oil is used for deep-frying as it reaches a high temperature before breaking down.

Olives (*Olive or ulive*)

Olives are a much-prized crop throughout Italy, picked from September when green, or left to ripen on the tree until purple, then black, and picked in winter. The flavour is dependent on the time they are picked. Fresh green olives are very acid and bitter and are pricked and brined before preserving in oil. Green and black olives suit different dishes and are not really interchangeable. They are of course crushed to make olive oil. Black and green olive pastes are rich and salty and can be used as toppings, bread and pasta flavourings or even whisked into a dressing.

Pasta, dried (*Pasta asciutta*)

Dried pasta can be made with (*all'uova*) or without egg. It is the staple food of southern Italy (from Naples downwards) where it is commercially made from durum wheat (*grano duro*) and water only. There are hundreds of shapes, all named differently according to regions, and there is even a Pasta Museum in Rome! Fresh pasta (*pasta fresca*) is made with eggs and soft wheat '00' flour and eaten mainly in the central regions, especially Emilia-Romagna. Choose a popular brand – there are so many to choose from – even organic!

Pepper (*Pepe*)

Black pepper is extensively used in northern cuisine due to the spice trade through Venice. It is always used freshly ground. It has crept into all Italian cooking now – except dishes with very delicate flavours. Never buy ready ground pepper though as it will be stale.

Polenta (*Farina gialla*)

This is coarsely ground maize or corn (*granoturco*) used to make either soft polenta 'porridge' served with rich meat sauces or the firmer sliced and grilled polenta, served with grilled and roasted meats and game. *Polenta bianca* or white corn meal is used in the Veneto and Friuli. It takes a good forty minutes to cook with continual stirring, but 'quick-cook or instant' polenta is ready in five to ten minutes and can be substituted, although the texture and flavour of real polenta is far superior. Polenta was the food of the poor in the north of Italy until enjoying today's global revival! Couscous is hand-rolled to this day from semolina flour and water, and is eaten in Sicily where it is steamed and eaten with a fish broth.

These bottles of vinegar, or aceti di vino, are produced from the Chianti region in Tuscany.

These large fresh olives, grown in Sicily, are displayed in a market stall in Trapani.

Preserved meats and sausages (*Salumi*)

Cotechino is large spiced fresh pork sausage often served as part of a *bollito misto* from Emilia-Romana. They are available vacuum-packed in good Italian delicatessens. Salami is handy for the larder although this is rarely used for cooking.

Italian sausages, or *salsiccie*, are freshly made at Italian delicatessens (and in pork butchers in Italy) and are made with coarsely ground pork (two-thirds lean and one-third fat) and highly seasoned with salt and pepper. They are often flavoured with fennel seeds, chilli, basil and pine kernels. They are perfect cooked on the barbecue, are firm, and have lots of flavour. Sometimes they aren't linked and are wound into a coil to be cooked whole in a frying pan (skillet) and then sliced. *Luganega* is the most famous type of *salsiccia*, originating from Lombardy.

Pancetta is unsmoked cured belly pork. There are two kinds – *pancetta stesa*, which is the whole piece or belly, and *pancetta arrotolata*, which is seasoned, spiced, rolled and sliced to order – it is a dry cure and smoked bacon should not be substituted. *Pancetta affumicata* is cured and smoked and very thinly sliced like streaky bacon.

Zampone is a stuffed pig's trotter that has been filled with minced pork and spices and is a speciality of Modena. Again this is sold vacuum-packed in Italian delicatessens.

Meats are being prepared in the salami and sausage curing room in Chianti, Tuscany.

Pulses and beans (*Legumi e fagioli*)

Borlotti, haricot, black-eyed, cannellini and *toscanelli* beans are staples throughout Italy, and are used in hearty soups, stews and simple salads. Many varieties of beans, both fresh and dried, are used in Italian cooking.

Fresh young broad (fava) beans (*fave*) are devoured raw in great piles in late spring with pecorino (romano), or *prosciutto crudo*. Dried *fave* are used throughout southern Italy during the winter to make various soups and purées.

Fresh *borlotti* are the beautiful red-marbled beans that sadly lose their colouring when cooked. All fresh beans have a lovely creamy texture when cooked and are packed with protein.

Dried chickpeas (*ceci*) are amongst the oldest foods still eaten in Italy – they are cooked in soups, salads and stews and must be well soaked before using. Do not buy stale ones – they will never cook!

Lentils (*lenticchie*) – the finest and smallest come from Castelluccio in Umbria – are eaten on New Year's Day for good luck. They are eaten with sausages (*salsicce*), *cotechino* and *zampone*. Generally they don't need soaking unless they are very old, but if so, soak them in cold water for about 5 hours or overnight and then drain and rinse.

Rice (*Riso*)

Rice is used in risottos, timbales, soups, salads, Sicilian *arancini* and Roman *supplì*. There are actually four types of rice grown in the Po Valley. *Ordinario* (short round grain used for desserts), *semifino* (medium length round grain for soups and salads), *fino* (an Italian long grain rice for everyday risotto making) and *superfino* (the best for risotto-making as it is rich in starch) – varieties include *arborio*, *vialoni nano*, *vialone nano gigante* and *carnaroli*. This type of rice has good absorption and plenty of starch – essential for making creamy risottos. *Vialone nano* and *carnaroli* hold their shape very well after cooking. *Arborio* tends to swell up more and should be treated with great care as it can disintegrate easily.

Risotto is a northern dish from Piedmont, Lombardy and the Veneto, though a type of risotto is made in southern Italy, deriving from Arab cuisine. It is made with boiled rice dressed with other ingredients and uses a less absorbent type of rice such as *ribe* or *originario*. The array of rice on an Italian supermarket shelf is astounding and it is worth keeping a large quantity and range at home!

Salt (*Sale*)

Salt is extremely important in the Italian kitchen. From ancient times it has been used to preserve food and it still is (for capers, anchovies, salt cod and more). Bread is unpleasant without salt – even in Tuscany – you have to be born there to appreciate the saltless bread (a result of high taxation in the past)! Pasta water is liberally salted to give the pasta flavour, and all fried food should be sprinkled with salt as soon as it comes out of the oil. Everything is seasoned during the cooking process so that the salt can penetrate deep into the food and release the flavour. Italian salt is sea salt, still made by the ancient method of evaporation in open salt pans. Fine salt (*sale fino*) is used for the table and baking, and coarse salt (*sale grosso*) used in cooking. Much of Italy's salt comes from Sicily where it is made in the same stone salt pans built by the Greeks. Near Marsala, there are huge white mountains of it protected by overlapping terracotta tiles.

Spices (*Spezie*)

The Romans used fennel and poppyseeds to flavour breads but it was during the Renaissance, when the Venetians were the centre of the spice trade with the East, that spices became widely used.

Cinnamon (*canella*), nutmeg (*noce moscato*), vanilla (*vaniglia*), aniseed (*anice*), black and white pepper (*pepe nero, bianco*), cloves (*chiodi di garofano*) and ginger (*zenzero*) were used to mask the taste of rotting food and as preservatives – they are all used today, especially in the Veneto, Siena (in *panforte*) and Sicily.

Juniper (*ginepro*) is prized in mountain country and in Rome. It is used in meat and game cookery.

Fennel seeds (*semi di finocchio*) and saffron (*zafferano*) grow wild in Sicily and are fundamental to the cuisine.

These vibrant red plum tomatoes in Palermo are superior in texture and taste in Italy and are an essential part of cooking for many regions.

Tomatoes (*Pomodori*)

Although only introduced from the New World in the sixteenth century, tomatoes have become an essential ingredient, especially in Naples and the south. They come in all shapes and sizes from long plum to cherry. Really ripe red tomatoes are used for sauce-making, whereas the greenish under-ripe tomatoes are eaten in refreshing salads. They are so cheap that people still bottle them whole and in sauce form for the winter.

Canned and bottled tomatoes are essential in the winter when fresh are not available – they are often better than most of the fresh tomatoes we see in other countries. They need the addition of a little sugar to correct the acidity, and to be well reduced. *Passata* is strained crushed tomato, thicker than tomato juice, but not nearly as thick as purée (paste). It can really pep up a sauce or stew.

Tomato purée or paste (*concentrato di pomodori*) comes in jars, cans and tubes and must be refrigerated once opened. This is essential to the store-cupboard to add a rich depth of flavour to sauces and stews.

Sicilian *estratto* or *strattu*, a clay-like sun-dried concentrate of puréed fresh tomatoes, is a real find – a little goes a long way and it keeps for months. Really ripe tomatoes are puréed and sieved, mixed with salt and lightly cooked. The thick sauce is then spread out over wooden boards and left to dry in the hot sun. The sauce is scraped and turned until it has turned to bright red 'clay'. It is then rolled into balls and kept under olive oil. Commercially made *estratto* is a reddish brown colour, and doesn't quite have the zing of the hand-made stuff. It is readily available in Sicilian markets – bring some back from your holiday (it keeps in the freezer too). Sun-dried tomatoes are used sparingly in Italian cooking. They originate from southern Italy and Sicily, where they are traditionally halved, salted and left in the sun to dry on woven fennel mats. They are also commercially dried. Look out for the reddest ones that are still flexible – they will have the most flavour. They are used to boost the flavours of sauces, soups and stews during the winter months. Their popularity has spread and they are now ubiquitous.

Truffles (*Tartufi*)

The white truffle (*tartufo bianco, tartufo d'Alba*) is the most prized for its pungent flavour and aroma and is eaten raw. The best come from the chalky soil of Piedmont, and they also can be found in the Crete Senese in Tuscany and in the Veneto. They are a creamy-beige colour, have a smooth outer surface and are a sort of misshapen ball shape. White truffle is often served shaved on a *risotto in bianco* or a *risotto Milanese*. Black truffles (*tartufo nero, tartufo di Norcia, tartufo di Spoleto*) come from Norcia or Spoleto in Umbria. They are also found in Le Marche, Veneto and Lombardy. The outside of the black truffle is rough, rather like the skin of a lychee, except dark brown or black. Inside it has a sort of marbled pattern in the dark flesh. Black truffles generally need to be cooked to release the flavour and are delicious cooked with eggs, cheese or used to dress pasta. Both types of truffle are sniffed out by

trained dogs or pigs, the owners holding them back whilst carefully digging out the buried treasure. Truffles can range from 2 to 20cm in diameter and are sold by weight. Fresh truffles are unbelievably expensive. When buying fresh truffles make sure you are not paying for a pocket of mud in the weight – truffles can have holes in them that fill up with earth! Apart from being sold fresh, they can be found preserved in jars, but these are nothing like the real thing and really not worth the money.

Truffle oil can liven up a salad, risotto or grilled meat, but it is very powerful and can take over if you use too much.

Truffle and mushroom paste is a great treat to mix into pasta or spread on toast or in little sandwiches.

Vinegar (*Aceto*)

Red wine vinegar is used in most Italian kitchens. It is used to give a sweet-sour flavour (*agrodolce*) to many dishes.

Balsamic vinegar (*Aceto balsamico*) is a rich sweet vinegar from Modena, made from the boiled-down must (*mosto*) of white Trebbiano grapes, aged in wooden casks for at least ten years and some of the best as much as sixty years. The price *does* reflect the quality – as the vinegar ages, it becomes richer and sweeter, and storing it costs money. Balsamic vinegar is especially good sprinkled on strawberries, and can enrich a sauce or dressing. There is no real substitute, but sherry vinegar reduced with a little sugar would do at a pinch. Cheaper versions made with vinegar and caramel are available but cannot be called *aceto balsamico tradizionale*.

The important moment when batches of Balsamic vinegar, or aceto balsamico *are tasted. These barrels have been produced in the Emilia-Romagna region.*

Truffles are highly valued and are carefully sought with the help of specially trained dogs. These ones are tartufi bianchi, *or white truffles.*

1
Antipasti

Stuffed courgette (zucchini) flowers

Zucchini ripieni

MAGGIE BEER teaches the preparation of this wonderful dish at her school in Tuscany. When in season, these flowers are a must for any selection of antipasti throughout Italy. They are particularly popular at weddings and grand receptions. When my friends Sara and Martin were married in a converted monastery in Piedmont, I ate the best-ever *zucchini ripieni*, lovingly prepared by the Scavia family's marvellous cook.

The dramatic male flower that grows on a long stalk from the centre of the courgette (zucchini) plant is best for stuffing – the female flowers produce the courgettes (zucchini), so picking these too soon is a waste! These gorgeous blooms are sold in bunches in Italian markets and are a very popular first course. They can be prepared in an elaborate way or be simply battered and shallow- or deep-fried. In fact, when absolutely fresh there is no need for any stuffing. Possible stuffings include finely chopped bocconcini *(tiny bite-sized* mozzarelle*) with anchovies, as used here; finely diced* mortadella *sausage mixed with garlic, breadcrumbs, parsley, freshly grated Parmesan and drops of olive oil; or fresh ricotta or goat's curd mixed with chopped spinach or silverbeet and seasoned with salt, pepper and nutmeg. MB*

MAKES 12

FOR THE BATTER OR *PASTELLA*:
250g/9oz/1⅔ cups plain (all-purpose) flour
1 teaspoon salt
120ml/4fl oz/½ cup olive oil
350ml/12fl oz/1½ cups warm water
2 egg whites

FOR THE STUFFING:
36 *bocconcini*
12 anchovies in oil
1 teaspoon dried oregano
black pepper
olive oil, for frying
12 courgette (zucchini) flowers
extra sea salt, for sprinkling

1 To make the batter, put the flour and salt into a bowl and make a well in the centre. Mix the olive oil with the warm water and tip into the flour. Work the batter until smooth, then leave it to rest for at least 1 hour.

2 Cut the *bocconcini* into quarters. Rinse the anchovies, pat dry and finely chop. Mix the chopped *bocconcini* with the anchovies and oregano. Season with black pepper but no salt.

3 Beat the egg whites until stiff and then fold these into the batter. Use the batter immediately.

4 Pour olive oil into a large saucepan or wok to a depth of 3cm/1¼in and heat. The oil will be hot enough when a tiny cube of bread dropped into it browns straight away.

5 Remove the pistils from inside the flowers. Place a spoonful of stuffing in each flower and gently fold the petals around it. Dip the stuffed flower in the batter, lightly shake off the excess, and then fry until golden brown. Drain very well on crumpled kitchen paper and serve immediately sprinkled with sea salt.

Sicilian chickpea and rosemary fritters

Panelle [v]

These are the ubiquitous Sicilian street food – little fritters made with ground chickpeas. I ate them in Menfi mercatino (little market) stuffed into a huge bun and smothered with some sauce! Home-made ones are much better – crispy on the outside and soft in the middle, but they must be served hot, and sprinkled with lots of salt.

MAKES ABOUT 40 (DEPENDING ON SIZE)

300g/11oz/2 cups chickpea flour (sold as
    gram flour or besan in Indian shops)
700ml/1¼ pints/3 cups water
2 tablespoons chopped rosemary
oil, for frying
salt and freshly ground black pepper

1 Lightly oil a cold surface such as a marble slab or the back of a large baking tray (sheet). Have a spatula at the ready.
2 Sift the chickpea (gram) flour into a saucepan. Whisk in the water slowly, making sure there are no lumps. Stir in the rosemary, salt and pepper to taste. Bring to the boil, beating all the time. Stir constantly until the mixture really thickens and leaves the side of the pan (like choux pastry). Don't worry if you get lumps – they will disappear when fried.

3 Now work really quickly – tip the mixture on to the oiled surface and spread it out as thinly and evenly as you can – about 3mm/⅛in. Leave to cool and set.
4 When set, cut into small triangles or squares and place between layers of cling film (plastic wrap).
5 Heat some oil in a wok or deep fat fryer. The oil is ready when a piece of mixture sizzles instantly when thrown in. Deep-fry a few at a time in the hot oil, turning when golden brown. Drain on kitchen paper, sprinkle with salt and serve hot.

Parmesan crisps

Parmigiano croccante [v]

A fairly recent and popular invention – you'll never make enough of these thin, crunchy savoury crisps – they are really more-ish! They can be made in a frying pan, but it is much easier to bake them in quantity in the oven. They keep well in an airtight tin.

SERVES 4

125g/4½oz/1 cup freshly grated Parmesan
a few fennel seeds (optional)
finely chopped fresh red chilli (optional)

1 Line a baking tray (sheet) with non-stick baking parchment. Spoon small mounds of cheese on to the paper at regular intervals. Flatten with the back of the spoon. Sprinkle a few fennel seeds or some chopped chilli on top if you like.

2 Bake in a preheated oven at 200°C/400°F/Gas 6 for 3–6 minutes until golden. Remove from the oven, leave for a couple of minutes to set (you can curl them over a wooden spoon or rolling pin at this stage), then carefully lift them off the paper. Cool completely before storing in an airtight container.

Balsamic figs grilled with prosciutto

Fichi alla griglia con aceto balsamico e prosciutto

I first ate this dish in a tiny restaurant perched high above Lucca. It was summer, and the food was prepared on an outdoor barbecue. The smell of the figs and ham cooking was as unforgettable as the view of the hills around us. This was an impromptu invention of the owner, and is something I cook all the time when good figs are in season. It's quick and easy, made with the simplest ingredients – but they must be of the best quality. The balsamic vinegar caramelizes on the figs, giving them a smoky sweet-and-sour flavour.

SERVES 4

8 fresh ripe figs
2 tablespoons balsamic vinegar
extra virgin olive oil (see method)
12 slices prosciutto
shaved Parmesan, extra virgin olive oil and
   crushed black pepper, to serve

1 Take each fig and stand it upright. Using a sharp knife, make two cuts across each fig, not quite quartering it but keeping it intact. Ease the figs open and brush with balsamic vinegar and olive oil.

2 Place the figs cut side down on the barbecue or griddle and cook for about 3–4 minutes until hot and slightly charred. Alternatively, place the figs cut side up under a really hot grill (broiler) until browning and hot through.

3 While the figs are cooking, place half the slices of prosciutto on the barbecue or griddle and cook until frazzled and starting to crisp. Remove and keep warm while cooking the remaining ham.

4 Arrange three pieces of prosciutto and two figs per person on warm plates. Cover with shaved Parmesan on each plate, drizzle with extra virgin olive oil and sprinkle with plenty of crushed black pepper.

Lady in white

Dama bianca [v]

VIANA LA PLACE, with her southern Italian origins, has a flair for making salads look as good as they taste. Combined with soft white mozzarella and crunchy celery, this recipe is a poem on the palate, and on the plate! Fennel is eaten raw in salads all over Italy. It must be sliced very thinly, and when marinated in a dressing, it softens and becomes easier to eat.

SERVES 4

450g/1lb fresh mozzarella
1 fennel bulb
1 celery heart, white sticks only
100ml/4fl oz/½ cup extra virgin olive oil
juice of 1 lemon
salt and freshly ground black pepper

This is a 'study in white' that originates from an Italian menu dating from the 1800s. Thinly sliced mozzarella, moist and tasting of fresh milk, is topped with slivers of crisp fennel and celery heart, then drizzled with extra virgin olive oil and lemon juice. Accompany this exquisite antipasto with a fine chilled white wine and breadsticks. VLP

1 If the mozzarella is packed in water, drain it well. Place mozzarella on kitchen paper to absorb excess water.
2 Cut off the feathery stalks of the fennel and trim away any bruised areas. Cut the bulb in half and remove the core. Slice the fennel into julienne strips. Cut the leafy tops off the celery. Trim the base and cut the celery crosswise into thin slices.
3 Cut the mozzarella into thin slices and arrange on a platter. Scatter the fennel and the celery over the top. Season with some salt and pepper to taste. Drizzle with the olive oil and lemon juice and serve immediately.

Grilled aubergine (eggplant) pickled with thyme, garlic and balsamic vinegar

Melanzane alla griglia marinate con timo, aglio e aceto balsamico [v]

STEPHANIE ALEXANDER makes this recipe in her classes in Tuscany and it has become one of her most popular dishes. Aubergines (eggplants) are pickled or marinated all over Italy when they are at the height of their season. Grilling them gives a deep smoky flavour. The lovely round aubergines (eggplants) are particularly good prepared as shown here.

SERVES ABOUT 15

750g/1lb 10oz aubergines (eggplant)
extra virgin olive oil (see method)
6 cloves garlic, thinly sliced
4 tablespoons roughly chopped fresh thyme
    (including stalks)
4 tablespoons balsamic vinegar
sea salt and freshly ground black pepper

This delicious pickle often forms part of an antipasto platter for dinner that includes our own preserved mushrooms and fresh ricotta made only that morning. We also eat it as the first course for lunch while still faintly warm, with borage flowers and rocket (arugula) picked wild from the fields. SA

1 Cut the aubergines (eggplant) lengthways into 1cm/½in thick slices, then cut the slices in half diagonally. Brush with a little olive oil.

2 Grill over coals or on a chargrill pan (even under an overhead grill or broiler), turning once. Transfer the aubergines (eggplant) to a bowl or a deep baking tray (sheet) and allow to cool a little. Scatter with the garlic, thyme, salt and pepper.

3 Mix the balsamic vinegar with 120ml/4fl oz/½ cup extra virgin olive oil. Pour two-thirds of this over the aubergine (eggplant) and turn to coat evenly, then leave to cool.

4 Pack the cooled aubergines (eggplants) into sterilized jars and pour over the rest of the vinaigrette. Shake the jars to release any pockets of air, then seal. This pickle is ready to eat straight away but will also remain delicious for several months.

Broad (fava) bean, pear and pecorino (romano) crostini

Crostini di fave, pere e pecorino [v]

In the spring, mounds of fresh young broad (fava) beans are on sale everywhere in Italy. In Tuscan alimentari *(local delicatessens), they will often be part of a proud window display, sitting resplendently on top of piled whole pecorino (romano) cheeses. They couldn't be simpler to eat – serve a pile of them still in the pod with slices of pecorino (romano) cheese and a little olive oil, of course! Eat the beans – raw – as you pod them, with the sharp cheese. I made a beautiful display of mounds of beans and plates of pecorino (romano) down the length of the dining-room table one evening in the Fattoria Montellucci, Pergine Valdarno – it looked stunning, but the guests were not convinced that this was the best way to eat them! If this is not your style, then try them as shown here – the flavours are still there.*

SERVES 6

one Italian *sfilatino* or small thin
   French baguette
extra virgin olive oil (see method)
250g/9oz/1⅓ cups shelled fresh broad
   (fava) beans
1 small ripe pear
balsamic or sherry vinegar
   (see method)
125g/4½oz pecorino (romano), salted
   ricotta or feta
salt and freshly ground black pepper

1 Slice the bread into thin rounds, brush with olive oil and spread out on a baking tray (sheet). Bake in a preheated oven at 190°C/375°F/Gas 5 for about 10 minutes until golden and crisp.

2 To prepare the beans, blanch them in boiling water for 3 minutes. Drain them and refresh in cold water. Using your fingers, pop them out of their skins.

Roughly mash them with a fork, moisten with a little olive oil and season well.

3 Core and finely chop the pear. Mix with a drop of balsamic vinegar. Finely cube the cheese and mix with the pear and vinegar.

4 Spread the *crostini* with a mound of bean purée and top with a spoonful of pear and cheese. Serve immediately.

Sardines to look like fig-peckers

Sarde alla beccaficu

The boned, rolled and stuffed sardines are said to look like the up-ended tails of little fig-peckers (birds) when assembled in the dish with their tails pointing skywards. Ready-prepared sardines are sold stacked in silvery piles in Sicilian fish markets, especially for this dish. Typical Sicilian ingredients are used here – sardines, orange, pine nuts, capers and currants – to give that balance of sweet and savoury, which reveals an Arabic influence. This is usually served as a light lunch dish or with other fish dishes as part of a main course.

SERVES 4

16 fresh sardines
50g/2oz/½ cup pine nuts, toasted
25g/1oz/¼ cup currants
3 tablespoons chopped fresh parsley
1 tablespoon salted capers, drained
    and chopped
finely grated rind (zest) and juice of 1 orange
150ml/¼ pint/⅔ cup good olive oil
a few fresh bay leaves
salt and freshly ground black pepper

1 Scale the sardines with the blunt edge of a knife. Cut off the heads and slit open the bellies. Remove the guts under running water. Slide your thumb along the backbone to release the flesh along its length. Take hold of the backbone at the head end and lift it out. The fish should now open up like a book.
2 Mix together the pine nuts, currants, parsley, capers, salt and pepper and orange rind (zest). Place a tiny spoonful on the flesh-side of each fish. Roll up from the head end and secure with a cocktail stick if necessary.
3 Oil a shallow dish. Place the rolled sardines in rows, tightly packed together, with their tails sticking upwards. Tuck the bay leaves in between the fish. Whisk together the orange juice and olive oil and pour over the fish. Season well and bake in a preheated oven at 200°C/400°F/Gas 6 for 10–15 minutes. Serve warm or at room temperature the next day.

Sautéed cracked olives

Olive fritte [v]

A delicious and easy way to serve otherwise bland olives – it dramatically improves their flavour. I was shown how to make these by an Italian friend from Calabria – her family has always treated olives this way – especially if the olives have been in brine too long. Serve these warm sautéed olives with ice-cold Martinis or cocktails like the famous Negroni.

SERVES 6

30 large black olives in brine, soaked overnight
    in water
olive oil
2 cloves garlic, finely chopped
1 tablespoon dried oregano
7 tablespoons red wine vinegar

1 Drain, rinse and dry the olives. Smash them lightly with the end of a rolling pin.
2 Heat enough olive oil to just coat the base of a heavy frying pan (skillet). Add the olives and swirl around the pan for 2 minutes. Add the garlic and fry for a couple more minutes. Sprinkle with oregano, pour over the vinegar, and swirl around the pan for another 2 minutes or until all the vinegar is driven off. Serve hot straight from the pan or warm.

Marinated (bell) peppers with artichokes and anchovies

Peperoni marinati con carciofi e acciughe

Roasted (bell) peppers make a good antipasto in themselves and are a classic throughout Italy. Artichoke hearts fit nicely into the cup-shaped halves. Salted anchovies have a much superior flavour to canned or bottled ones in oil. Usually, they are whole and have to be rinsed, split open and the backbone and other small bones removed – much easier than it sounds.

SERVES 6

6 red, orange or yellow (bell) peppers
12 preserved artichoke hearts in oil, drained
24 anchovy fillets in oil, drained or 12 salted
   anchovies, cleaned, bones removed
   and rinsed
4 cloves garlic, sliced
2 tablespoons chopped fresh oregano or
   1 tablespoon dried
good olive oil, for drizzling
2 hard-boiled (hard-cooked) eggs,
   finely chopped
salt and freshly ground black pepper

1 Place the whole (bell) peppers in a grill pan and roast under a preheated grill (broiler) or on the barbecue, until the skin begins to char. Turn the peppers until they charred all over. Don't be tempted to halve the peppers to grill them or they will lose all their juices. Place in a plastic bag to steam for 5–10 minutes.

2 Peel off the skins whilst warm. Cut the (bell) peppers in half lengthways through the stalks and remove the seeds. Place the peppers cut side up in a shallow dish.

3 Halve the artichokes and place two halves in each (bell) pepper half. Lay two anchovy fillets over the artichokes. Season well with salt and pepper. Scatter over the sliced garlic and oregano.

4 Drizzle the (bell) peppers with olive oil. Cover and refrigerate overnight for the flavours to develop. Serve at room temperature sprinkled with the chopped hard-boiled egg.

Deep fried sage leaves

Foglie di salvia fritte

This dish was first tasted at a friend's wedding in Piedmont and creates a real taste explosion. It may seem fiddly, but it is a delicious appetiser to have with drinks. The leaves can be dipped in batter singly, or can be sandwiched together with an anchovy and caper paste.

MAKES 12

24 large sage leaves
1 teaspoon salted capers, rinsed
1 tablespoon anchovy paste

FOR THE BATTER (*PASTELLA*):
1 egg
150ml/¼ pint/⅔ cup iced water
125g/4½oz/1 cup plain white
   (all-purpose) flour

1 Wash and dry the sage leaves. Mash the capers with the anchovy paste and spread on to the darker green side of the leaves. Press another leaf on top to form a sandwich.

2 Lightly whisk the egg and iced water together. Add the flour and whisk into the egg and water, leaving it a bit lumpy. Do not allow to stand, but use immediately.

3 Heat the oil in a deep pan or wok until a piece of stale bread dropped in turns golden in a few seconds. Holding the leaves by the stem, dip into the batter and lightly shake off the excess. Drop a few at a time into the hot oil, and fry until crisp and barely golden. This will only take a few seconds. Drain on kitchen paper and serve straight away.

Golden flower artichokes

Carciofi fritti [v]

VIANA LA PLACE produces superb vegetable dishes, and this is her special method for crispy golden artichokes. Artichokes are cooked and eaten all over Italy, and you learn to prepare them at your mother's (or grandmother's) knee. They are an essential part of Italian life from late spring to late summer. A huge variety are seen in markets – the smallest are eaten whole, and the larger ones need their tough leaves and chokes removing before cooking.

SERVES 4

1 lemon, cut in half
8–12 medium artichokes
olive oil, for frying
salt to taste

Large, tender artichokes fried in hot olive oil are a feature of cooking in the Jewish quarter of Rome. In this dish, which is a version of the Roman recipe, baby artichokes are gently pounded until the leaves open up like flowers. They are fried in olive oil until the exterior leaves turn crunchy and golden brown and the heart and the interior leaves become meltingly tender. A dusting of salt is the only seasoning required. VLP

1 Fill a big bowl with water and squeeze in the juice of half a lemon. Use the other lemon half to rub the cut portions of the artichoke as you work. Trim the artichokes by snapping back the dark green outer leaves. Trim away the dark green portions at the base and trim the stalk. Cut about 1cm/½in off the tops of the leaves. As you work, place each artichoke in the acidulated water.
2 Drain the artichokes and dry them well. Pound each artichoke against a hard surface, head down, until the tightly clenched leaves open up like a flower.
3 Pour enough olive oil into a medium frying pan to give a depth of at least 1cm/½in. When medium hot, fry the artichokes in the oil a few at a time, pressing them down to open up the leaves. Use tongs to turn the artichokes in the oil and brown them on all sides. Cook slowly for about 5 minutes, raising the heat toward the end of the cooking to brown the exterior of the artichokes. Lift them out of the pan and let excess oil drain back into the frying pan. Drain the artichokes on kitchen paper and season with salt to taste. Transfer the artichokes to a platter and serve immediately.

2

Soups

Quadrucci pasta in broth

Quadrucci in brodo

GIULIANO BUGIALLI is a renowned master of pasta-making, and he also demonstrates here the importance of a good quality broth in Italian cuisine. Soups come in many forms, the purest being a good clear broth with a few additions such as pasta. The pasta here is home-made and it reveals beautiful green parsley leaves that are used inside the parcels through the golden depths of the soup.

SERVES 8

FOR THE BROTH:

900g/2lbs dark turkey meat, with bones
1 medium-sized red onion, peeled
1 stick celery
1 medium-sized carrot, scraped
1 medium-sized clove garlic, peeled but
    left whole
1 cherry tomato
4 sprigs Italian parsley
3 extra large egg whites
coarse-grained salt

FOR THE PASTA:

40g/1 ½ oz/½ cup freshly grated Parmesan
5 eggs
pinch of salt
6 twists black pepper
450g/1lb/3½ cups plain (all-purpose) flour
30 sprigs Italian flat-leaf parsley, leaves only

A few herbs as well as spices may be added to pasta dough. Pasta containing whole fresh parsley leaves is a representative dish from Puglia. Other herbs are chopped very finely before they are added to the dough, but with parsley it is traditional to add the whole leaves, probably because the chopping would discolour them. Besides, the attractive pattern they produce is reason enough to use the leaves whole. This dough has another special feature: the grated cheese is mixed into the dough itself rather than sprinkled on the cooked pasta. Most pasta in this region is eaten without the addition of grated cheese. The parsley pasta is usually cut into the square-shaped quadri *or* quadrucci, *of varying size. They are usually eaten in turkey broth, with a lamb sauce or with melted butter and sage leaves. The shape of* quadrucci *and the use of broth rather than sauce accentuate the beauty of the whole-leaf pattern of the pasta, which almost resembles embroidery. GB*

1 Prepare the broth: put the turkey, coarse-grained salt to taste, the whole onion, celery, carrot, garlic, tomato, and parsley sprigs in a large stockpot. Cover with cold water and put the pot over medium heat, uncovered. Simmer for 2 hours, skimming off foam from the top.

2 Remove the meat from the pot and reserve it for another dish. Pass the rest of the contents of the pot through a fine strainer into a large bowl, to remove the vegetables and impurities. Let the broth cool, then place the bowl in the refrigerator overnight to allow the fat to rise to the top and solidify.

3 Use a metal spatula to remove the solidified fat then clarify the broth. Pour 4 tablespoons of the broth into a small bowl and mix it with the egg whites. Pour the broth and egg white mixture into the rest of the cold broth and whisk very well. Transfer the broth to a pot and place it on the edge of a burner. Bring to the simmering stage, half covered, and simmer for 10 minutes, or until the egg whites rise to the top with the impurities, and the broth becomes transparent.

4 Meanwhile, place a clean, wet cotton tea towel in the freezer for 5 minutes. Then stretch the tea towel over a colander and strain the broth through it to clarify it completely. The broth should be absolutely clear.

5 Prepare the pasta with the ingredients listed, placing the grated Parmesan, salt, pepper, and eggs in the well in the flour, and following the directions in the recipe for Cannelloni with broad (fava) beans and ricotta (see page 59).

6 Stretch the pasta as thinly as possible by hand or with the pasta machine. Place the whole parsley leaves on top of half the length of the layer of pasta. Fold the other half of the layer of pasta over the parsley, and press the layers together. Continue to roll out the layer of pasta until it is very thin. Using a scalloped pastry cutter, cut the pasta into squares of about 5cm/2in.

7 Bring the broth to a boil and add the pasta. Cook for 1–3 minutes, depending on how dry the pasta is. Serve hot, without adding cheese, which would spoil its purity.

Iced tomato and (bell) pepper soup with salsa verde

Zuppa fredda di pomodoro e peperoni con salsa verde

The secret of this soup relies on really good full-flavoured sun-ripened tomatoes to conjure up the taste of southern Italy. Adding the salsa verde gives a sweet-and-sour flavour, common to the south of Italy and Sicily. Though salsa verde originates in the north, and is usually served with bollito misto, I have taken the liberty of serving it with this soup to produce a great contrast of flavours. The serving of cold soups is a legacy of the Spanish occupation of Sicily.

SERVES 6

900g/2lbs fresh ripe red tomatoes
(vine ripened) or Italian canned
chopped tomatoes
2 large red (bell) peppers, halved, cored
and seeded
2 cloves garlic, skinned and chopped
1 small red chilli, seeded and finely chopped
600ml/1 pint/2½ cups fresh tomato juice or
passata (strained crushed tomato)
6 tablespoons extra virgin olive oil
2 tablespoons balsamic vinegar
salt and freshly ground black pepper

FOR THE SALSA VERDE:
2 cloves garlic, finely chopped
4 anchovy fillets in oil, rinsed
3 tablespoons each chopped fresh parsley,
mint and basil
2 tablespoons salted capers, rinsed
and chopped
150ml/5fl oz/⅔ cup extra virgin olive oil
2 tablespoons freshly squeezed lemon juice
salt and freshly ground black pepper
600ml/1 pint/2½ cups crushed ice, to serve

1 Remove the core from the tomatoes with a small sharp knife. Plunge the tomatoes into boiling water for about 5–10 seconds, remove and refresh in cold water. Slip off the skins. Cut in half around the middle and gently squeeze out the seeds. Place in a food processor.
2 Roughly chop the red (bell) peppers and add to the tomatoes with the garlic and chopped chilli. Blend to a rough purée. Transfer to a bowl and stir in the tomato juice, olive oil and balsamic vinegar to taste. Season with salt and pepper, then cover and chill overnight to allow flavours to develop.

3 Meanwhile, make the salsa verde. Pound 1 teaspoon salt and the garlic in a pestle and mortar until creamy. Stir in the remaining ingredients and season with pepper. Transfer to a glass jar and pour a layer of olive oil on top to exclude the air. This will keep for up to a week in the refrigerator.
4 Stir the crushed ice into the soup and serve with a bowl of the salsa verde to stir into the soup.

Clam and courgette (zucchini) soup

Aquacotta di mare

I learned to make this soup whilst visiting a friend in Tuscany, who sees cooking as a kind of alchemy that comes from the heart, through the mix and balance of good ingredients. This is a typical light fresh soup made more substantial by ladling over toasted bread.

SERVES 4

750g/1lb 10oz fresh baby clams in shell, or
   cockles, cleaned
3 tablespoons olive oil plus extra
1 large clove garlic, finely chopped
750g/1lb 10oz courgettes (zucchini)
finely grated rind (zest) and juice of 1 lemon
1 tablespoon chopped fresh marjoram
1 litre/1¾ pints/4 cups vegetable stock (broth)
   (see page 49)
6 thick slices country bread, toasted
1 large clove garlic, peeled and bruised
salt and freshly ground black pepper

1 Steam the clams until they open. Reserve the juice and remove half the clams from their shells, keeping half the clams in their shells for a garnish.
2 Heat the olive oil in a saucepan and add the garlic. Cook gently until golden but not brown. Slice the courgettes (zucchini) thickly and add them to the pan with the lemon rind (zest) and marjoram and turn in the oil and garlic. Pour in the stock (broth), season lightly and bring to simmering point. Cover and simmer for 10 minutes, until the courgettes (zucchini) are soft.

3 Pass through a coarse food mill and return to the pan. Add the reserved clam juice and the shelled clams. If the soup is too thick, add extra stock (broth) or water. Taste and season with salt and pepper and a little lemon juice. Stir in the clams in their shells.
4 To serve, rub the toasted bread with garlic, place a slice in each bowl and ladle on the soup. Drizzle each serving with olive oil and serve immediately.

Roasted pumpkin and garlic soup

Crema di zucca e aglio arrosto [V]

Pumpkin is so popular in Italy and makes wonderful smooth soups. Roasting the pumpkin and garlic together in this recipe, from Milan, concentrates the flavour of the pumpkin and gives a sweet nutty flavour to the garlic. Look for a variety with bright orange dense flesh.

SERVES 6–8

750g/1lb 10oz fresh pumpkin
6 cloves garlic, left unpeeled
4 tablespoons olive oil
2 medium onions, finely sliced
2 celery sticks, chopped
50g/2oz/¼ cup long grain white rice
1.5 litres/2½ pints/7 cups vegetable (or
   chicken stock (broth) (see page 49)
4 tablespoons chopped fresh parsley
salt and freshly ground black pepper

1 Scrape out the seeds from the pumpkin, cut off the skin and cut into large cubes. Place in a roasting tin (pan) with the garlic cloves and toss with 2 tablespoons olive oil. Do not crowd the pan – use two tins if necessary. Roast in a preheated oven, 200°C/400°F/Gas 6 for about 30 minutes until very tender and beginning to brown.
2 Heat the remaining olive oil in a large saucepan and add the onion and celery. Cook over a gentle heat for 10 minutes until just beginning to brown and soften.

Stir in the rice, pour in the stock (broth), bring to the boil, cover and simmer for 15–20 minutes until the rice is tender.
3 Remove the pumpkin from the oven, cool slightly, then pop the garlic cloves out of their skins. Add the garlic and pumpkin to the saucepan, bring to the boil and simmer for 10 minutes. Blend and return to the pan. Taste and season with freshly ground black pepper. Add extra stock (broth) or water if the soup is thick. Reheat to serve and stir in the parsley.

Meat soup 'married' with vegetables and cheese

Minestra maritata

GIUSEPPE SYLVESTRI's recipe comes from a tradition of 'big' soups, which are very important to Italian cooking, especially in large families. These soups are nutritious and filling and were also cooked to feed hungry workers at midday, although like many other peasant dishes, they have now become fashionable – in smaller portions – in restaurants. The long, slow cooking process is important to extract the full flavour from the simple but best quality ingredients.

SERVES 8–10

1 escarole, shredded
½ Savoy cabbage, shredded
1 head of chicory (Belgian endive), core
   removed and shredded
1 *cavolo nero* (Tuscan black
   cabbage), shredded
1 bunch broccoli tops, or spring
   greens, shredded
1 bunch kale, shredded
4 tablespoons olive oil
2 small lamb shanks
2 veal shanks
1 guinea fowl (guinea hen), cut up into
   small joints
2 pieces fresh Italian sausage
100g/4oz streaky bacon, diced
100g/4oz pecorino (romano), cubed
100g/4oz Parmesan, cubed
salt and freshly ground black pepper

Maritata comes from the Neapolitan dialect for the word married. For this reason, you will find several different varieties of vegetable, meat and cheese 'married' together in this soup. Illustrating the differences between the cooking of the regions in Italy, this is the Neapolitan version of the well-known Tuscan soup ribollita. *Traditionally, this is a winter soup, made in large quantities to last throughout the week. Although there are many versions of this soup, this is my favourite – my sister's version. Traditionally it is eaten with an Italian dried bread called* freselle, *which can be found in most Italian delicatessens. GS*

1 Wash and chop all the vegetables. Put the vegetables into a large pan with 3 tablespoons of olive oil. Mix well, then cover and let the vegetables 'sweat' for 10 minutes. Drain and set aside.
2 In another large saucepan or stockpot, add the remaining olive oil, brown the meat in batches, removing them to a plate as you go. Return all the browned meats to the pan and completely cover with water. Bring to the boil, then turn down the heat and simmer for ½ hour, topping up with water as necessary. Add the vegetables (and more water if needed) and simmer gently for another hour.
3 Stir in the cheeses. Simmer for another 10 minutes. Season with salt and plenty of freshly ground black pepper. Cover and let the soup stand for at least 15 minutes before eating.

Tomato and bread soup

Pappa al pomodoro [v]

MAGGIE BEER's recipe is one of the most important dishes in Tuscan cooking. The Tuscans are never wasteful and left-over bread plays a big part in the cuisine. Their food is simple, but made with the best ingredients to hand – even if that is only bread and tomatoes. If the tomatoes are bursting with sunshine, the combination is incredible.

There have been times after days of teaching and eating, when I felt I couldn't eat another thing. On one such day, we went to a restaurant in Siena recommended by a friend. At first I was a little disappointed, as the waiters were formally dressed and were fluent in English, and there were lots of tourists. Not in the mood for food, I ordered pappa al pomodoro *– and all my uncertainty fled. It was as simple, rustic and perfumed as I could have hoped. I poured a 'C' of peppery, green extra virgin olive oil over the surface as the Tuscans do, and I was revived! This soup is as good as its ingredients: great tomatoes, good bread and wonderful, green olive oil. Using left-over bread is typical of Tuscan resourcefulness. MB*

SERVES 8–10

1kg/2¼lbs really ripe tomatoes
2 cloves garlic, finely chopped
extra virgin olive oil (see method)
1 small handful fresh basil leaves, coarsely
    chopped or torn
1 litre/1¾ pints/4 cups chicken or vegetable
    stock (broth) (see page 49)
500g/1lb 2oz day-old bread, crusts removed
freshly grated Parmesan
salt and freshly ground black pepper

1 Remove the stalks from the tomatoes, wash, halve, remove the seeds and roughly chop them.

2 Briefly sauté the garlic in a little olive oil in a large saucepan, then add the tomatoes and basil and grind in some pepper. Cook for 5 minutes, then season with salt.

3 Add the stock (broth) and gently bring to simmering point. Cut the bread into 1cm/½in cubes, add to the pan and cook for a few minutes, stirring. Cover the pan and simmer over a low heat for 30 minutes.

4 Taste and adjust the seasoning, then ladle into bowls, drizzle each with 2 tablespoons olive oil and serve hot, warm or cold (but never chilled). Offer the Parmesan separately.

Chestnut and pancetta soup

Minestra di castagne e pancetta

I made this robust and chunky soup after gathering fresh sweet chestnuts with my friends Antonella, Anna and Emiliano in the Chianti hills one October afternoon. Preparing the chestnuts is a bit of a chore, but the flavour and texture is wonderful. If fresh chestnuts are not available, use dried (available from good delicatessens and Italian stores), or even soaked dried chickpeas.

SERVES 6

750g/1lb 10oz fresh, plump, sweet chestnuts
    or 400g/14oz/about 2 cups dried
    chestnuts, soaked overnight in cold water
125g/4½oz/8 tablespoons butter
150g/5oz pancetta or streaky bacon, chopped
2 medium onions, finely chopped
1 carrot, chopped
1 stick celery, chopped
1 tablespoon chopped fresh rosemary
2 fresh bay leaves
2 cloves garlic, halved
salt and freshly ground black pepper

1 Using a small sharp knife, slit the shell of each chestnut across the rounded side. Put the chestnuts into a saucepan and cover with cold water. Bring to the boil and simmer for 15–20 minutes. Remove from the heat and lift out a few chestnuts. Peel off the outer thick skin, then peel away the inner thinner skin (this has a bitter taste).

2 Melt the butter in a large saucepan and add the pancetta or bacon. Fry over a medium heat until beginning to turn golden. Add the chopped vegetables and cook for 5–10 minutes until beginning to soften and brown.

3 Add the chestnuts to the pan with the chopped fresh rosemary, fresh bayleaves, halved garlic cloves and enough water to completely cover. Bring to the boil, half cover, turn down the heat and simmer for 30–45 minutes, stirring occasionally. The chestnuts should start to disintegrate and thicken the soup. Taste and season well.

Tuscan white bean soup with garlic and chilli oil

Zuppa di toscanelli con aglio tostato e olio infuso al peperoncino [V]

This is my version of the famous Tuscan soup made from the much-prized toscanelli *beans. This is a thick, warming peasant soup. The beans are cooked with water for simplicity, but made with chicken stock (broth), it has a much deeper flavour.*

SERVES 4

250g/9oz/1⅓ cup dried white beans (haricot,
    toscanelli), soaked overnight in cold water
a handful fresh sage leaves
4 cloves garlic
150ml/¼ pint/⅔ cup really good olive oil
2 tablespoons fresh sage or rosemary
1 teaspoon dried red chilli flakes
salt and freshly ground black pepper
roughly chopped fresh parsley, to garnish

1 Drain the beans. Place in a flameproof casserole. Cover with cold water to a depth of 5cm/2in above the beans, and push in the sage. Bring to the boil, cover tightly and bake in a preheated oven 170°C/325°F/Gas 3 until tender (1 hour).

2 Finely chop half the garlic, and thinly slice the remainder. Put half the beans, the sage, and all the liquid into a blender until smooth. Pour back into the casserole. Add water or stock (broth) if too thick.

3 Heat half the olive oil in a frying pan and add the chopped garlic. Fry gently until soft and golden. Chop and add the herbs and cook for 30 seconds. Stir into the soup and reheat until boiling. Simmer gently for 10 minutes. Taste and season. Pour into a heated tureen or soup bowls.

4 Fry the sliced garlic in the remaining olive oil until golden, add the chilli flakes and spoon over the soup. Serve sprinkled with chopped fresh parsley.

Fish stew from Le Marche

Brodetto

FRANCO TARUSCHIO is from Le Marche and knows the cuisine inside out. He has presided over his legendary Walnut Tree restaurant in Wales for many years, often putting soups like this on the menu made with locally caught fish. Although many know the region of Le Marche for game and mushroom dishes, it has a coastline too. This soup is made from the fruits of the sea, and similar soups can be found in all the coastal areas around Italy.

SERVES 6

1.6kg/3lbs fish, a mixture of red mullet, monkfish, whiting, gurnard, sole, mussels and Dublin Bay prawns (large shrimp) as available – you can ask the fishmonger to clean them for you
425g/15oz squid
1 onion, very finely chopped
1 clove garlic, crushed
3 tablespoons extra virgin olive oil
6 ripe plum tomatoes, peeled, seeded and chopped
150ml/5fl oz/⅓ cup dry white wine
a little white wine vinegar
425g/15oz/1¾ cups tomato passata (strained crushed tomato)
3 tablespoons finely chopped parsley
salt
toasted country bread, to serve

For centuries this was the dish the fishermen made to use up the fish not wanted by their customers. It evolved into a more refined but still robust dish over the years. There are many ways of preparing this dish and great arguments are to be heard as to which is the best – with saffron or without? … and so it goes on. Originally brodetto *always had thirteen different types of fish, corresponding to the number of people who were present at the Last Supper. Fewer can be used, but never twelve, as this is considered to be an unlucky number, a reminder of the traitor Judas. It is amusing to see the fish restaurants along the coastline with signs saying 'Vincenzo il mago', the wizard of the* brodetto, *or 'Carlo, il rè', the king of the* brodetto! *In fishing seaside resorts, like Porto Recanati, the fishermen are to be seen bringing their catch in very early in the morning and selling it directly to the housewives and chefs at the quayside or in their own shops. No housewife or chef buys fish after 10 o'clock in the morning and whatever is left is sold off cheaply. No tired fish there. This is how we served* brodetto *at the restaurant in Wales. FT*

1 Clean the fish and cut into largish chunks. Clean the mussels and prawns (shrimp) but do not shell the prawns. Discard any mussels that are damaged or open. Clean the squid and slice finely.

2 Fry the onion and garlic in olive oil in a shallow pan (preferably one with two handles) until golden. Add the squid to the pan and cook for 3–4 minutes. Stir in the chopped tomatoes, wine and a few drops of vinegar, the tomato passata and a little salted water to the pan. After a few minutes, add 2 tablespoons chopped parsley, then the prawns (shrimp) and the thicker pieces of fish.

3 Leave to cook a few minutes, then add the remaining fish and the mussels. Cover the pan and cook over a medium heat for about 5 minutes until the fish and mussels are done, shaking the pan gently from time to time so that the fish does not stick.

4 Remove the pan from the heat and leave to rest, covered with the lid, for 2–3 minutes.

5 Serve sprinkled with the rest of the parsley and pieces of bread toasted on the griddle.

Fennel and lemon soup with black olive gremolata

Crema di finocchio e limone con gremolata di olive nere [v]

Raw bulb, or Florence fennel, lemon and ripe black olives are a perfect marriage of flavours. To give this a summery flavour, use the fat salad onions (scallions) and crinkled baked olives for a fruity flavour. Fennel's aniseed flavour is essential to southern Italian cooking.

SERVES 4

5 tablespoons olive oil

a small bunch of spring onions (scallions)

250g/9oz fennel, trimmed and cored

1 large potato, peeled and diced

finely grated rind (zest) and juice of 1 lemon

1 small clove garlic, finely chopped

finely grated rind (zest) of 1 lemon

4 tablespoons chopped fresh parsley

16 Greek black olives, stoned and chopped

750ml/26fl oz/3¼ cups stock (broth)
  (see below)

salt and freshly ground black pepper

1 Heat the oil in a large saucepan and add the onions. Cook for 5–10 minutes until beginning to soften. Thinly slice the fennel, reserving any green fronds for the *gremolata*, and add to the pan with the potato and lemon rind (zest), and cook for 5 minutes until the fennel begins to soften. Pour in the stock (broth) and bring to the boil. Turn down the heat, cover and simmer for about 25 minutes or until tender.

2 For the *gremolata*, finely chop the garlic, lemon rind (zest), reserved fennel and parsley and mix. Add the olives and mix into the mixture. Cover and chill.

3 Liquidize and pass the soup through a sieve to remove any strings of fennel. The soup should not be too thick. If it is, add some more stock (broth). Return to the rinsed-out pan. Reheat, taste and season well with salt, pepper and a really good amount of lemon juice. Sprinkle each serving with the *gremolata*, which is stirred in before eating.

Basic stock (broth)

Brodo

MAKES ABOUT 2 LITRES/3½ PINTS/8 CUPS

2 onions, 2 large carrots and 2 sticks celery,
  all peeled and roughly chopped

2 leeks, chopped and washed thoroughly

a handful parsley stalks

2 bay leaves, 1 sprig fresh rosemary, 1 sprig
  fresh thyme, tied into a bouquet garni

2 tablespoons sunflower oil

salt and freshly ground black pepper

FOR THE CHICKEN STOCK (BROTH):

2–3 raw chicken carcasses

FOR THE FISH STOCK (BROTH):

4 kg/9lb bones and heads non-oily fish, gills
  removed, 1 bottle dry white wine and
  4 garlic cloves

1 Place all the vegetables and the bouquet garni in a large pan with the oil. Cook over a medium heat for 10 minutes until the vegetables begin to soften and lightly colour. Season and cover with 4 litres/7 pints/18 cups water.

2 Bring to the boil over a high heat, skim, turn down the heat to medium and cook for 1 hour. Allow to cool, strain through a sieve and return to the rinsed pan.

3 Bring to a rolling boil until reduced by half. Taste and season. Cool, cover and chill or freeze.

TO MAKE CHICKEN STOCK:

Cut the chicken into large pieces. Place in a large pan, cover with cold water and bring to the boil over a high heat. Remove the scum. Add the vegetables (omit the bouquet garni and oil) and simmer over a low heat. After 2 hours, pour through a fine sieve. Return to the pan, boil and skim. Continue as for step 3.

TO MAKE FISH STOCK:

Chop the fish and place in a large pan with the vegetables (omit the bouquet garni and oil) and cover with the wine and enough water to cover. Simmer gently for 45 minutes, skimming twice. Strain into a clean pan, boil and continue as for step 3.

Ligurian vegetable soup with pesto sauce

Minestrone con pesto [v]

CLAUDIA RODEN has travelled the length and breadth of Italy gathering recipes for many books and television series. This soup captures the essence of what a real minestrone is.

SERVES 6–8

1 slice (about 250g/9oz) pumpkin, or a few
   sliced courgettes (zucchini)
4 medium potatoes, peeled and diced
1 small cauliflower, broken into small florets
75g/3oz mushrooms, roughly chopped
100g/4oz fresh or frozen peas
150g /5oz broad (fava) beans, or green
   beans, cut in pieces
400g/14oz can cannellini beans, drained
   and rinsed
1 onion, finely chopped
2–3 tablespoons olive oil
6 ripe tomatoes, peeled and chopped,
   or 1 x 400g/14oz can plum tomatoes
3 tablespoons finely chopped parsley
100g/4oz/½ cup rice or pasta (ribbons or
   broken tagliatelle)
pesto (see recipe below)
4 tablespoons grated Parmesan or
   pecorino (romano)
salt and freshly ground pepper

FOR THE PESTO SAUCE:

2 cloves garlic, crushed
50g/2oz/½ cup pine nuts
50g/2oz basil weighed with the stems
   (or 8 supermarket bunches)
4 tablespoons grated pecorino (romano)
   sardo or Parmesan
150ml/¼ pint/⅔ cup light olive oil
salt

The cooking of Liguria depends much on vegetables and herbs and not on the fruits of the sea as one might expect. Ligurians adore herbs and greenery: they cook everything with their delicate olive oil, one of the best in Italy. All Liguria's traffic and exchanges were made across the sea: it received pine nuts from Pisa, pecorino (romano) cheeses from Sardinia and salted anchovies from Spain. This is the kind of soup which is best made the day before to give the flavours time to mingle – don't worry about the long cooking time as the vegetables are meant to disintegrate and thicken the soup. Pesto sauce, which accompanies this soup, is the prince of Ligurian dishes and is also ideal serve with trenette, tagliatelle, corzetti or gnocchi. CR

1 Dice the pumpkin and add it to a large saucepan with the potatoes, cauliflower, mushrooms, peas and broad (fava) beans (you can skin them if you like). Cover completely with cold water, bring to the boil, the turn down the heat, and simmer for about 40 minutes or until the vegetables are very tender. Add the cannellini beans and heat through.
2 In the meantime, fry the onion in oil until soft, add the tomatoes and parsley and cook a further 5 minutes, then pour the mixture into the soup and check the seasoning.
3 20 minutes before serving, bring the soup back to the boil and add the rice, or add the pasta 10 minutes before serving. When the rice or pasta is cooked, stir in the pesto, or pass it around along with the grated cheese and let everyone help themselves.

Pesto sauce

1 To make the pesto sauce, pound the garlic and pine nuts in a large mortar with a little salt. Add the chopped basil leaves (it may seem a lot, but the flavour of basil outside Italy is often less perfumed), a few at a time, pounding and grinding the leaves against the sides of the bowl. You can also put everything in a food processor or blender.
2 Now stir in the grated cheese and mix very well, then gradually beat in the olive oil (the olive oil of Liguria is very light, delicate and perfumed).

3

Pasta
and Sauces

Slow-cooked tomato and meat sauce

Sugo di ragù

MARY CONTINI has a wonderful family-run Italian delicatessen in Edinburgh, Scotland, which now boasts a busy restaurant. Like many Scottish Italians, she cooks the way her grandmother taught her, passing on the old ways to younger generations, but adding her own lighter touches. Her recipe for a slow-cooked meat sauce is essential to the Italian way of life. Spalebone is a piece of meat from under the shoulder blade, which requires long, slow cooking. (In the US, the cut is an oval piece of meat that comes from underneath the blade in the chuck). It is very flavourful.

SERVES 8–10

3 tablespoons extra virgin olive oil
1 medium-sized onion, very finely chopped
a small piece dried chilli
250g/9oz piece of spalebone beef (a muscle in the shoulder)
1 clove garlic, peeled and chopped
a handful flat-leaf parsley, finely chopped
5 x 400g/14oz cans good quality Italian tomatoes
sea salt

As a child, my favourite day was Sunday. We always collected my nonna *(grandmother) to take her with us to Mass, then, afterwards, one or two of my brothers and sisters were allowed to stay with her for lunch. There were eight of us, so competition was fierce. In her house, life revolved around the kitchen. The morning was taken up preparing lunch. Firstly, a pot of* sugo *was prepared, and then left on a low heat to cook slowly for about 2 to 3 hours. The lid was always balanced on a wooden spoon placed over the pot, so that the* sugo *would reduce very slowly and the wonderful aroma would fill the whole kitchen. Anticipation for lunch was increased by a succession of tasks, culminating in the grating of the pecorino (romano). This ridged, dull yellow-rinded sheep's cheese was sent over in sealed packages from* nonna's *home in Picinisco – a tiny hamlet high in the Abruzzo mountains. Grating the pecorino (romano) was hard for my small hands but as I was positively encouraged to enjoy as much of the pungent, creamy cheese as I worked, this was always a task I relished. MC*

1 Warm the extra virgin olive oil in a heavy-bottomed saucepan. Add the chopped onion and the dried chilli, stir it around and sauté it very slowly until the onion is soft and transparent. (This is called a *soffrito* and is the basis of many recipes in Italian cooking.)
2 Meanwhile, cut a few slits in the spalebone with a sharp knife and push a little garlic and parsley into each slit.
3 Turn the heat up and add the spalebone to the saucepan, browning it on each side.
4 Smooth and de-seed the tomatoes by passing them through a food mill (mouli-legumes) or a fine sieve.

5 Add the tomatoes to the meat, bring to a slow simmer and cook for 2–2½ hours with the lid balanced on the pot with a wooden spoon as described above. When the *sugo* has reduced by about a third season it to taste with sea salt.
6 Serve with chunky pasta such as *rigatoni* or *penne rigate* and sprinkle with freshly grated pecorino (romano) or Parmesan. The spalebone becomes very tender and delicious and is eaten after the pasta – but before the main course!

Neapolitan Sunday meat sauce

O'Zuffritto

GIUSEPPE SYLVESTRI's recipe for another slow-cooked meat sauce shows how different they can be. This one has a variety of meats in it and is quite hot with chilli. They both rely on unhurried cooking.

SERVES 8–10

one ham shank

450g/1lb shoulder of pork

250g/9oz belly pork

450g/1lb shoulder of veal

50g/2oz bacon fat (this is fundamental to the flavour – but you could use olive oil)

3 bay leaves

2 tablespoons mild chilli paste

150g/5oz/½ cup tomato purée (paste)

1 litre/1¾ pints/4 cups beef stock (broth) (see page 49)

salt and freshly ground black pepper

cooked pasta, to serve

This is one of the recipes that make us understand the importance of foreign influences on the cooking of Italy. Zuffritto is derived from the era of Spanish domination in Naples, and is a good example of the differences and great variety we experience throughout Italian regional cooking. I come from Capri, an island eighteen miles off the coast of Naples. Yet one will not find zuffritto on any Caprese table – it is a Neapolitan dish. In fact, a Neapolitan friend, who wanted me to taste something 'from home', introduced the sauce to me. We all love to share our ideas and cooking. The combination of meats is important here to get the right flavour – the method is simple, but the secret of success is in the long, slow cooking process. GS

1 Remove the bone from the ham shank and cut away the skin. Carefully chop all the meats into really small cubes.

2 Melt the bacon fat in a heavy pan. Turn the heat to low and add the chopped meats. Turn the meat around in the pan and fry for about 10 minutes until sealed. Stir in the bay leaves.

3 Add the chilli and tomato purée (paste) and continue to cook until it has a dense consistency. Add the beef stock (broth), bring to the boil then simmer for at least 1 hour until the sauce is reduced by half and the meat is tender. Season with salt and pepper. Serve with *rigatoni* or *ziti*.

Wild mushroom and pesto lasagne

Lasagne al forno con funghi e pesto

This is a wonderfully rich and robust dish from the area around Tuscany, Umbria and Le Marche where wild mushrooms abound and fresh egg pasta is still made. Ordinary mushrooms can be used, but use flavoursome, dark, open-cap mushrooms or field mushrooms. Do not be tempted to use shitake mushrooms – they are completely the wrong flavour. This takes time to make, but it really is worth it!

SERVES 6

FOR THE MUSHROOM SAUCE:

25g/1oz dried porcini (ceps or *boletus edulis*)
900g/2lbs fresh wild mushrooms (porcini, ceps or field mushrooms)
4 tablespoons good olive oil
125g/4½oz/8 tablespoons butter
1 medium onion, chopped
4 cloves garlic, peeled and chopped
4 tablespoons chopped fresh parsley
2 or 3 sprigs fresh thyme, chopped
300ml/½ pint/1¼ cups meat or chicken stock (broth) (see page 49)

FOR THE PESTO:

3 cloves garlic, peeled
75g/3oz/¾ cup pine nuts
75g/3oz/2 cups fresh basil leaves
250ml/8fl oz/1 cup good olive oil
75g/3oz/6 tablespoons unsalted (sweet) butter, softened
4 tablespoons freshly grated Parmesan
salt and freshly ground black pepper

2-egg quantity pasta dough (see Cannelloni recipe [page 59] for making fresh pasta)
freshly grated Parmesan and extra butter, to finish

1 First make the mushroom sauce. Cover the dried mushrooms with warm water, sit a saucer on top and leave to soak for 20 minutes. Brush or wipe the fresh mushrooms clean and thinly slice them. Drain the soaked mushrooms, reserving the soaking liquid. Squeeze the mushrooms gently and roughly chop.
2 Heat half the oil in a large sauté pan and add the butter. When foaming, add half the fresh and dried mushrooms and half the chopped onion and sauté over a high heat for 4–5 minutes until tender and beginning to soften. Repeat with the remaining half, then combine the two batches in the pan, stir in the chopped garlic, parsley, and thyme, cook for a further 2 minutes.
3 Next, pour in the stock (broth) and reserved dried mushroom liquid, bring to the boil and boil rapidly for 4–5 minutes until the sauce reduces and turns syrupy. Leave aside to cool.
4 To make the pesto, put the garlic in a pestle and mortar with a little salt and the pine nuts. Pound until broken up. Add the basil leaves, a few at a time, pounding and mixing to a paste. Gradually beat in the olive oil, little by little, until the mixture is creamy and thick. Beat in the butter and season with pepper, then beat in the cheese. Alternatively, put everything in a blender or food processor and process until smooth. Store in a jar with a layer of olive oil on top to exclude the air, in the refrigerator until needed.
5 Roll the pasta very thin (see Fresh Pasta recipe for Cannelloni [page 59]), cut it to the size of your dish, laying it on a clean, flour-dusted cloth as you proceed. (This will allow the pasta to dry a little and prevent it sticking together when cooking.)
6 Bring a large pan of salted water to the boil and drop in a few pasta sheets at a time. When the water comes back to the boil, the pasta is cooked. Lift it out and drain over the sides of a colander.
7 Butter a 23 x 30 x 5cm/9 x 12 x 2in ovenproof dish, and line with a layer of pasta. Cover this with a layer of pesto, another layer of pasta, then mushroom sauce, a layer of pasta and repeat these layers until all is used up, finishing with a final layer of pasta. Dredge this with grated Parmesan and dot with any remaining butter. Cover with oiled kitchen foil and bake at 180°C/350°F/Gas 4 for 20 minutes. Uncover, then bake for a further 20 minutes until golden. Allow to stand for 10 minutes before serving.

Spaghettini with chilled tomato sauce

Spaghettini con salsa di pomodori cruda [v]

MARY CONTINI presents another classic recipe here which shows how to make a simple sauce from raw tomatoes – although you must first find the best and most flavoursome. The warmth of the cooked pasta will bring out their flavour.

SERVES 4–6

500g/1lb 2oz of the sweetest tomatoes
2 tablespoons extra virgin olive oil
1 clove new season's garlic, peeled and finely sliced
a large handful fresh basil leaves
sea salt
cooked spaghettini, to serve

This is a summer recipe for hot clammy days: it relies on the very best, sweetest tomatoes, which must be very ripe and very red. Luckily, Italian stem-ripened tomatoes are widely available now. This recipe comes from my husband's Neapolitan nonna (grandmother). Of course she had the advantage of a constant supply of the very best San Marzano tomatoes. In less warm climes, leave your tomatoes on a sunny window ledge for a couple of days until they are really ripe. MC

1 Wash the tomatoes and remove the stalks. Skin them by plunging them in boiling water for a couple of minutes, then into cold water. If they are ripe enough, the skin will slide off easily with the help of a slit down the side of each tomato with a sharp knife.

2 Chop them roughly, put them into a sterile (preserving) jar and add the extra virgin olive oil. Add the sliced garlic, tear the basil into pieces and add this to the tomatoes. Season with salt and mix well. Cover and refrigerate overnight.

3 Warm the sauce gently for about 10 minutes, just to take the chill from it (or leave at room temperature for 20 minutes) and serve on spaghettini, cooked *al dente*.

TIP: No cheese is served with this sauce – the fresh flavour of tomatoes and basil is mouth-watering enough!

Cannelloni with broad (fava) beans and ricotta

Cannelloni con fave e ricotta [v]

URSULA FERRIGNO spends a lot of time researching food in southern Italy. She is especially fond of lighter vegetable dishes, and this cannelloni is an example of this, with lots of flavour. *Besciamella* sauce is fundamental to much Italian cooking, and Ursula guides you through the method with ease.

SERVES 6

FOR THE FRESH PASTA:

150g/5oz/1 cup Italian '00' or plain
    (all-purpose) flour
150g/5oz/1 cup fine semolina (durum) flour
a pinch of sea salt
1 tablespoon olive oil
2 large free-range eggs

FOR THE FILLING:

1 kg/2lb 4oz broad (fava) beans, shelled
350g/12oz/1 ½ cups ricotta
100g/4oz/1 ⅓ cups pecorino (romano), grated
1 large clove garlic, peeled and crushed
a large handful mint, chopped
sea salt and freshly ground black pepper

FOR THE *BESCIAMELLA* SAUCE:

600ml/20fl oz/2 ½ cups milk
2 slices of onion
1 bay leaf
1 blade mace
3 bruised parsley stalks
5 whole black peppercorns
50g/2oz/4 tablespoons butter
150ml/5fl oz/1 ⅔ cups white wine
40g/1 ½ oz/1 ⅓ cup plain (all-purpose) flour
sea salt and freshly ground black pepper
extra grated pecorino (romano), to serve

Broad (fava) beans and ricotta make this the lightest, freshest cannelloni dish you'll ever taste. It is from southern Italy, a place where the food is fresh and lively and where I am always glad to return. UF

1 To make the pasta, heap the flour and the semolina into a circle on the work surface. Sprinkle over the salt and mix well. Hollow out a well in the centre into which you break the eggs. Add the olive oil and, with much care and patience, gradually work the eggs and oil into the flour until you have a slab of dough. Shape this into a ball and leave under a towel or in cling film (plastic wrap) to rest while you prepare the filling.

2 Meanwhile boil or steam the broad (fava) beans until tender – for about 10 minutes. Drain and leave to cool. Once cool put half the beans in a food processor and pulse, leaving some texture. Add the ricotta, garlic, mint, pecorino (romano) and salt and pepper to taste. Add the remainder of the whole broad (fava) beans and mix well with a wooden spoon.

3 Roll out the pasta dough wafer thin and cut into squares of 8 x 8cm/3 x 3in, sprinkle lightly with semolina and allow to dry on a tray for 10–15 minutes. Once almost dry, cook the pasta squares in boiling, salted water. Drain when cooked but still firm to the bite.

4 Pre-heat the oven to 200°C/400°F/Gas 6. To make the *besciamella*, place the milk in a pan with the onion slices, bay leaf, mace, parsley stalks and peppercorns. Heat over a medium-low heat and bring to a simmer, remove form the heat and leave to infuse for 8–10 minutes.

5 Melt 30g/1oz/2 tablespoons butter in a saucepan and stir in the flour, then stir over the heat for one minute, remove from the heat and strain in the infused milk and mix well. Return the saucepan to the heat and stir or whisk continuously until boiling. Add the remaining butter and wine and simmer for 3 minutes. Season with salt and pepper to taste.

6 On each cooked pasta square spread one tablespoon of the broad (fava) bean filling and roll up into a cylinder. In a casserole or baking dish line with half of the *besciamella* sauce, place the filled cannelloni and layer with the remaining *besciamella*, sprinkle with extra grated pecorino (romano) cheese and bake in the pre-heated oven for 15–20 minutes. Serve immediately with extra pecorino (romano) cheese if you like.

Cheese and herb-stuffed ravioli from Capri

Ravioli Caprese

GIUSEPPE SYLVESTRI's ravioli are simple with a lightness expected from southern cuisine. His eggless pasta is so simple and very unusual – almost reminiscent of Chinese dim-sum paste.

I always begin my cooking lessons by telling my students to start with good ingredients. This is a classic example of that principle from my native island, Capri. The dish looks very simple on the face of it, but it is the use of local, fresh, quality ingredients, used in the old traditional way, which makes it memorable. The pasta contains no eggs, which makes it lighter, and it is rolled out by hand. In fact, London-based renowned chef Marco Pierre White asked me for the recipe when he tasted it! GS

SERVES 6

FOR THE PASTA DOUGH:
500g/1lb 2oz/3⅓ cups Italian "00" or plain (all-purpose) flour
about 175ml/6fl oz/¾ cup warm water
1 tablespoon olive oil
pinch of salt

FOR THE FILLING:
300g/11oz firm *caciotta* cheese, grated (use a very young pecorino (romano) if you can't find *caciotta*)
2 tablespoons chopped fresh marjoram
1 whole egg
2 egg yolks
100g/4oz/1 cup grated Parmesan
salt and freshly ground black pepper

FOR THE TOMATO SAUCE:
2 tablespoons olive oil
½ onion, diced
two pork or beef ribs
500g/1lb 2oz/2 cups Italian canned, peeled tomatoes
12 leaves of fresh basil

1 To make the dough, sift the flour on to a clean surface and form a mound. Make a well in the centre with your fist and add the warm water and olive oil. Mix together and work the dough on a flat surface until you get an elastic consistency (if it is a little dry, add some more water). The dough will be ready when you press it with your finger and it springs back. Put the dough in a warm place and cover with a clean tea towel.

2 To make the filling, simply mix all the ingredients together. Taste and adjust the seasoning. Set aside.

3 Roll out the dough on a floured surface as thinly as possible. (You may have to resort to a pasta machine!) Put a teaspoon of filling on the dough every 5cm/2in, until you fill one half of the sheet of pasta.

Leave the other side empty. Now fold the empty side over the filling. Press down between the ravioli, taking care to push out any trapped air. Cut into round shapes with a pasta – or biscuit (cookie) cutter.

4 To make the sauce, heat the oil in a saucepan and add the onion. Fry for 5 minutes until softened. Meanwhile, cut the meat from the bones and chop finely. Add the meat to the onion and brown well. Add the canned tomatoes, then the basil, torn into strips. Simmer for 15 minutes over a low heat. Pass the sauce through a sieve or food mill (mouli-legumes) and keep warm.

5 Meanwhile, cook the pasta in plenty of boiling salted water. As soon as they rise to the surface, they are ready. Drain well then toss with the meat and tomato sauce.

Macaroni and aubergine (eggplant) timbale

Sformato di maccheroni e melanzane

ALVARO MACCIONE is a passionate, intuitive chef who cooks with a big heart. He is a proud Tuscan who is not averse to cooking dishes from other regions … here he has an excuse! *Sformati* and *timballi* are very popular in the south of Italy in particular, and Alvaro will guide you through each step here with ease.

SERVES 8

3 large aubergines (eggplants)
olive oil (see method)
50g/2oz/4 tablespoons butter
100g/4oz/1 cup dried breadcrumbs
500g/1lb 2oz dried macaroni pasta
400g/14oz/1²/₃ cups *ragù* sauce (see page 54)
150g/5oz/2 cups grated Parmesan
1 teaspoon dried oregano
1 tablespoon chopped fresh basil

I am married to a Sicilian and spend much time in Sicily from where this dish originates. A sformato *is cooked in a deep dish lined with breadcrumbs, then turned out. You could alternatively use a springform tin (pan). AM*

1 Preheat the oven to 200°C/400°F/Gas 6. Slice the aubergines (eggplants) lengthways, and pan fry in a large frying pan with enough olive oil to coat the base until golden brown. In a deep ovenproof dish (terracotta type) rub the butter around the bowl, covering the inside completely, and then sprinkle and cover the butter with the breadcrumbs.

2 Line the dish with the aubergine (eggplant) slices lengthways, overlapping the rim. You will have some left over. Keep these to cover the filling.

3 Boil the macaroni until nearly *al dente*, drain and mix with the *ragù* sauce and Parmesan cheese. Taste, season and stir in the oregano and the basil.

4 Spoon the pasta into the lined dish up to the rim of the bowl. Flip the overhanging aubergine (eggplant) over the filling. Using the remaining slices, cover the remaining pasta evenly.

5 Set on a tray and bake in the oven for 25 minutes. Take the dish out of the oven and let it stand for about 10 minutes. Then place a plate on the top of the bowl and turn it upside down. Lift off the dish – the *sformato* should turn out easily. Serve the dish immediately.

TIP: Although there are many shapes of aubergine (eggplant), the long ones are more suitable for this recipe. Use the round ones for salads.

An eighteenth-century pasta dish

Vincisgrassi

FRANCO TARUSCHIO's greatest and most renowned dish is elaborate to prepare, but perfect for a special occasion.

SERVES 6

FOR THE FRESH PASTA:
500g/1lb 2oz/scant 4 cups Italian '00' or
    plain (all-purpose) flour
2 whole eggs, plus 4 egg yolks
1 teaspoon salt

FOR THE SAUCE:
150g/5oz/10 tablespoons butter
50g/2oz/¼ cup plain (all-purpose) flour
1.2 litres/2 pints/5 cups milk, heated
400g/14 oz fresh porcini (ceps or *boletus
    edulis*), sliced
4 tablespoons extra virgin olive oil
200g/7oz Parma ham, cut into julienne strips
200ml/7fl oz/scant 1 cup single (light) cream
3 tablespoons finely chopped parsley
150g/5oz/2 cups freshly grated Parmesan
salt and freshly ground black pepper
truffle oil, or if possible a little shaved
    white truffle

Vincisgrassi is a speciality of the Marche region of Italy where I was born, in particular of Macerata. The story goes that it was named after an Austrian general – Windisch Graetz, who was with his troops in Ancona in 1799 during the Napoleonic War. However, it was Antonio Nebbia, who wrote a gastronomic manual in 1784, that first mentioned a similar dish called Princisgras, *which is possibly its predecessor. FT*

1 Make a dough from the Fresh Pasta recipe (see Cannelloni on page 59), knead well and roll through a pasta machine as you would for lasagne. Cut the pasta lengths into squares approximately 12.5cm/5in square. Cook the squares in plenty of boiling salted water a few at a time. Place on linen tea cloths to drain.
2 To make the sauce, melt 50g/2oz / 4 tablespoons of the butter, add the flour and blend in well. Add the warm milk, a little at a time beating well with a balloon whisk. Cook the porcini in the olive oil and add to the sauce. Stir in the Parma ham. Add the cream and parsley, season to taste, and bring to the boil. Remove from the heat.

3 To assemble the *vincisgrassi*, butter a gratin dish and cover the bottom with a layer of pasta, then spread over a thin layer of sauce, dot with butter and sprinkle with some Parmesan cheese. Continue the process, making layer after layer, finishing with a layer of sauce and a sprinkling of Parmesan cheese.
4 Bake in a preheated oven at 220°C/425°F/Gas 7 for 20 minutes. Allow to stand for 10 minutes before serving. Serve with a little truffle oil splashed on top or, better still, with shavings of white truffle, and a little Parmesan cheese.

Spinach roll

Rotolo di spinaci [v]

FULVIA SESANI is famous for making pasta using egg yolks only. Indeed, every chef has their own method for this basic yet essential part of Italian cooking and it is these personal secrets that we look for from the masters.

SERVES 8

FOR THE FRESH PASTA:

about 225g/8oz/2 cups plain (all-purpose) flour, sifted

3 tablespoons extra virgin olive oil

3 tablespoons dry white wine

3 egg yolks

3–4 tablespoons water

1 egg yolk, for brushing pasta

FOR THE FILLING:

225g/8oz fresh spinach, blanched, chilled in ice water and liquid squeezed out

225g/8oz/1 cup ricotta

4 tablespoons melted butter

40g/1½oz/½ cup grated Parmesan

salt

This is my way of preparing pasta dough, by using just the egg yolk as I believe the whites make pasta tough. I then add oil for elasticity, wine to make it strong, and no salt so that the pasta does not hold too much moisture and become wet. FS

1 In a food processor place flour, oil, wine, and egg yolks; process and add the water one spoon at the time, until it forms a kind of granulated mixture like a couscous. Tip out on to a pastry board and knead by hand until the dough is smooth – this takes about 5 minutes.

2 Using a pasta machine, stretch the dough through the last notch to about 30 x 15cm/12 x 6in. Arrange 3 pieces on a clean tea towel and brush the long sides with a little egg yolk. Lay them side by side, overlapping each by 1.25cm/½in to make a pasta rectangle, 90 x 45cm/ 36 x 18in.

3 In a food processor, place the spinach and the ricotta, process for a few seconds, add salt to taste and remove the mixture to a pastry bag without a tip.

4 Spread the mixture on the pasta sheet, brush the edges right and left with the yolk and roll it up with the help of the towel underneath. Pinch the edges of the roll to hold in the spinach mixture and tie the ends with string.

5 Fill a fish pan or kettle with cold water, bring to a boil, add salt then carefully lower in the roll. Cook gently for about 30 minutes. Remove the roll from the water on to a pastry board, cut the strings and unwrap it. Slice thickly and arrange on a platter, drizzle with the melted butter and sprinkle with the Parmesan. Serve.

Chickpea pasta with prawns (shrimp), garlic and tomatoes

Pasta di ceci con gamberi, pomodori e aglio

I developed this dish when teaching in Villa Ravidà, Menfi, Sicily where it has become a firm favourite. Sicilians use chickpea (gram) flour to make little fritters called panelle *(see page 28) and not really much else. I knew that a form of chickpea pasta was made in southern Italy, served with fish or seafood – so here it is with a sauce of all that is good, fresh and local to Menfi. This pasta is very delicate, and is better rolled out slightly thicker than for normal tagliatelle. When cooking, don't stir too much or it will break up – handle it gently. It is ready when the salted water comes back to a rolling boil.*

SERVES 6

FOR THE FRESH PASTA:

175g /6oz/1¼ cups chickpea (gram) flour

500g/1lb 2oz/3⅓ cups Italian "00" or plain
   white (all-purpose) flour

1 teaspoon salt

5 large eggs

FOR THE SAUCE:

3 tablespoons extra virgin olive oil

4 cloves garlic, finely chopped

1 teaspoon dried chilli flakes

250ml/8fl oz/1 cup dry white wine

500g/1lb 2oz ripe tomatoes, peeled
   and chopped

1 teaspoon sugar (optional)

675g/1½lb small raw, prawns
   (shrimp) unshelled

4 tablespoons finely chopped flat-leaf parsley

salt and freshly ground black pepper

1 First make the pasta. Follow the instructions for making fresh egg pasta for Cannelloni (see page 59), but sieve the two flours together first. Roll out and cut into tagliatelle. Hang up to dry.

2 Put a very large pan of water on to boil with at least 1 tablespoon of salt in it. Heat the oil in a wide pan and add the garlic, fry until just golden then add the chilli and wine. Turn up the heat and boil fast to reduce the wine to almost nothing. Add the tomatoes (and the sugar if you like, to counter any acidity) and cook for 1–2 minutes until starting to 'melt'. Stir in the prawns (shrimp) and bring to the boil. Simmer for 2–3 minutes. Stir in the parsley, taste and season. Set aside.

3 Throw the pasta into the boiling water, stir well and keep over a high heat. It is ready when the water returns to the boil. Drain the pasta, reserving a ladleful of water in the pan. Mix the pasta with the water then the sauce. The water helps the sauce cling to the pasta. Serve immediately.

Pasta with sardines and wild fennel

Pasta con le sarde

ANNA TASCA LANZA teaches Sicilian cuisine on her estate in Sicily. This is one of the most important dishes in the cuisine, combining fish with a sweet-sour flavour, so common throughout the Mediterranean.

SERVES 10

FOR THE PASTA SAUCE:

1 onion, minced

2 cloves garlic, mashed

200ml/7fl oz/1 cup olive oil

450g/1lb wild fennel, blanched, drained and finely chopped

3 salted anchovies or sardines, rinsed and boned

1 litre/1¾ pints/4 cups thin tomato sauce

1 tablespoon *estratto* or sun-dried tomato purée (paste), dissolved in:

120ml/4fl oz/½ cup white wine

125g/4½ oz/½ cup dried currants

125g/4½ oz/½ cup pine nuts

450g/1lb fresh sardines, boned (see page 34)

salt and ground hot (chilli) pepper (or *peperoncino*)

FOR THE PASTA TOPPING:

75g/3oz/¾ cup fresh breadcrumbs

50ml/2fl oz/¼ cup olive oil

2 tablespoons sugar

2 tablespoons thin tomato sauce

1 clove garlic, mashed

125g/4½ oz/1¼ cups chopped parsley

800g/1lb 12oz *bucati* or *bucatini* pasta

salt and ground chilli pepper

In Sicilian cuisine, wild fennel has a thousand uses. It is one of the most popular and traditional ingredients on our tables. It costs nothing – just pick it anywhere. In the fall, when it is time for the olives to be cured, we dip the olives in brine and cover the containers completely with fennel fronds. We often use the seeds in bread dough. Our fresh pork sausage is traditionally seasoned with fennel seeds. Pasta con le sarde is the Sicilian national dish, and this is a variation made by a promising young chef called Walter in the town of Vallelunga near Regaleali. ATL

1 To make the sauce, sauté the onion and the garlic in the olive oil and add the fennel and anchovies. After the anchovies have dissolved, mix in the tomato sauce and tomato purée (paste), the white wine, currants, pine nuts, salt and chilli pepper. Simmer for about 30 minutes. Add the sardines and cook for 10 minutes more; they will break up while cooking.

2 For the topping, toast the breadcrumbs in a frying pan, mixing in the olive oil, sugar, tomato sauce, garlic, salt, and chilli pepper. Stir constantly, without burning the breadcrumbs, until they are a nice amber colour and crunchy to the bite. Serve them in a dish sprinkled with the chopped parsley.

3 To cook the pasta, bring a large pan of water to the boil. Add a good handful of salt. Add the pasta, stir and cook for about 8 minutes or until slightly softer than *al dente*. Drain the pasta, reserving a ladle or two of the water. Pour half of the sauce in the pan, add the pasta, and stir to coat completely. Pour into a serving dish and cover with the rest of the sauce, using the water if needed. This is the only pasta that improves if it sits for 5 minutes. Serve with the breadcrumb topping on the side.

4

Risotto, Polenta and Gnocchi

Polenta and wild mushroom bake

Polenta pasticciata [V]

FRANCESCO ZANCHETTA prepares his classic polenta recipe here, layering it in a baking dish with wild mushrooms. Polenta is like porridge but is made from yellow maize meal. It takes a long time to cook and needs constant stirring. It is then poured out on to a board, shaped into a mound and left to set, before cutting up to fry or bake.

SERVES 6

300g/11oz/scant 2 cups polenta (maize meal) flour
500g/1lb 2oz mixed wild mushrooms or porcini (*boletus edulis*)
1 white onion
3 tablespoons olive oil
a little vegetable or meat stock (broth) (see page 49)
3 tablespoons chopped fresh parsley
200g/7oz Taleggio cheese
200g/7oz/2 cups grated Parmesan
200g/7oz Fontina cheese
50g/2oz/4 tablespoons butter
salt and freshly ground black pepper

Polenta is an important staple from northern Italy. This is also a good recipe for using up any polenta left over from the night before. FZ

1 Prepare the polenta by slowly pouring the flour into 1 litre/1¾ pints/4 cups of salted, boiling water. Cook for 45 minutes on a low heat and then turn out on to a wooden board and leave to cool and set.
2 Meanwhile, clean and cut the mushrooms, finely chop the onion and fry in a little olive oil. Add the mushrooms and cook until ready using a little stock (broth). Season and add some parsley.

3 Cut the polenta into 1.25cm/½in slices and lay one layer in a oiled baking tray (sheet). Cover with half of the mushrooms, the Taleggio and half of the Parmesan cheese. Cover with another layer of polenta, add the rest of the mushrooms, the Fontina, the remaining Parmesan and a little butter. Bake at 180°C/350°F/Gas 5 for 40 minutes until brown and bubbling.

Grilled (broiled) polenta with Gorgonzola

Polenta alla griglia con Gorgonzola [v]

MAGGIE BEER's recipe for grilled (broiled) polenta is unusually made with milk instead of water for extra richness. Polenta is often served this way, as a substitute for cheese or a sauce.

At the cooking school in Tuscany, instead of cutting our polenta cake into wedges, as described here, we put the whole thing, dotted with Gorgonzola, into a hinged grill for easy turning over the coals, and then cut it into wedges to serve. While milk is not usually added to polenta, I find that it produces a wonderfully creamy, rich result. MB

SERVES 6

1 litre/1¾ pints/4 cups milk
700ml/1¼ pints/3 cups water
350g/12oz/ scant 2 cups polenta
  (maize meal) flour
50g/2oz/4 tablespoons unsalted (sweet)
  butter (optional)
100g/4oz/1⅓ cups freshly grated
  Parmesan (optional) or Gorgonzola
  (see method)
3 tablespoons olive oil
salt and freshly ground black pepper

1 In a heavy-based saucepan, bring the milk and water to a boil and add 1 heaped teaspoon of salt. Gradually pour in the polenta in a slow stream, stirring continuously with a wooden spoon. Once it has all been added, turn down the heat. Continue stirring so that a skin does not form. (Cooking the polenta slowly prevents it from being bitter.) The polenta will thicken and fall away from the sides of the pan. Remove the pan from the heat and season with pepper. Stir in the butter and cheese (this stage can be left out if you want the polenta to be less rich). Tip the polenta into a large baking tray and pat it out with wet hands until it is 2.5cm/1in thick, then leave until completely cold.

2 Preheat a grill (broiler) or chargrill pan. Cut the polenta into the desired shapes and brush with olive oil.
3 Put the oiled pieces of polenta on to the lightly oiled cooking surface and leave them alone. Polenta releases itself from the surface once it has formed an adequate crust and can then be readily turned without leaving the crust behind on the grill!

FOR GRILLED (BROILED) POLENTA WITH GORGONZOLA:
Instead of adding Parmesan to the cooking polenta, once set, cut the polenta into wedges, then dot each wedge with Gorgonzola and return them to the fire or grill (broiler) to heat through and melt.

Savoury prune and potato gnocchi

Gnocchi alle prugne [v]

FRANCESCO ZANCHETTA is a chef from the Trentino area, who enjoys researching and cooking medieval recipes especially from the Veneto and the north. This ancient recipe for a savoury potato *gnocchi* stuffed with prunes is one of them.

SERVES 6–8

FOR THE *GNOCCHI*:

1kg/2¼lbs potatoes (a yellow variety)
50g/2oz/½ cup soaked and pitted prunes
350g/12oz/2 cups plain (all-purpose) flour
2 eggs
½ teaspoon ground nutmeg
100g/4oz/8 tablespoons unsalted
 (sweet) butter
salt
extra flour, for dusting

FOR THE SAUCE:

5 shallots
100g/4oz/1 cup shelled walnuts
2 tablespoons olive oil
1 sprig rosemary, finely chopped
1 sprig thyme, finely chopped
4 tablespoons sweet white wine
salt and freshly ground black pepper
grated pecorino (romano), to serve

This is a typical northern Friuli dish. It is one of my favourites, very rich in flavours and quite unusual. It can be prepared with raw grated potatoes, but the traditional way of making gnocchi *makes it easier to produce. FZ*

1 Wash and scrub the potatoes. Place them in a pot with cold water and bring to boil. This step is important, as the potatoes need to cook with the skin intact, so they don't absorb too much of the water.

2 Cut the prunes into small pieces and set aside. For the sauce, peel and chop the shallots, chop the walnuts. Heat the oil and add the shallots, cooking for 5 minutes until softened. Stir in the walnuts, rosemary and thyme. Season with salt and pepper, add the wine and bring to the boil. Boil for 1 minute to evaporate the alcohol and set aside to cool.

3 Once the potatoes are cooked, drain carefully and peel immediately. Mash them into a large bowl, add the flour, the eggs, the nutmeg, the butter, and seasoning. Knead the ingredients very quickly and when the mixture has become smooth, cut into four pieces.

4 Dust the table with flour and roll a piece of mixture into a 2.5cm/1in thick sausage and cut into 1.25cm/½in pieces. Stuff each one with a piece of prune, roll into a little flour and set aside on a tray. Repeat until all the mixture is used.

5 Heat up the sauce, boil some of the *gnocchi* in plenty of salty water until they surface, which only takes a few minutes. Don't cook too many *gnocchi* at one time or they will stick together. Drain, then toss and reheat in the sauce for a minute and serve with some grated pecorino (romano) cheese.

Lemon-scented spinach and ricotta gnocchi

Malfatti con limone [v]

These are the lightest form of gnocchi, especially when made with snowy white, fresh ricotta as sold in Italian delicatessens. Malfatti means 'badly formed' – the less you handle them the lighter they are, so odd shapes don't matter! Ricotta is made from whey left after making either cow's milk or sheep's milk cheese. The ricotta sold in tubs in supermarkets is made from pasteurized cow's milk. Although these gnocchi are light, they are very filling!

SERVES 4

675g/1½lbs fresh spinach, or 300g/10oz
    frozen spinach, thawed
25g/1oz/2 tablespoons butter
1 shallot, finely chopped
finely grated rind (zest) of 1 lemon
150g/5oz/⅔ cup fresh ricotta, sieved
75g/3oz/scant ½ cup plain white
    (all-purpose) flour
2 egg yolks
75g/3oz/1 cup freshly grated Parmesan
freshly grated nutmeg
salt and freshly ground black pepper

FOR THE SAUCE:
2 lemons
175g/6oz/12 tablespoons unsalted
    (sweet) butter
2 fresh bay leaves
freshly grated Parmesan, to serve

1 Remove the stalks from the fresh spinach and wash the leaves in several changes of cold water. Drain well and place in a large pan. Cook until just wilted, cool slightly then squeeze out most of the moisture. Chop roughly and set aside. Squeeze the moisture out of the frozen spinach and roughly chop.

2 Melt the butter and fry the shallot until golden. Stir in the spinach and lemon rind (zest), and cook for a couple of minutes until coated and mixed with the butter and shallot. Tip into a bowl.

3 Beat in the ricotta and flour, egg yolks and Parmesan. When well mixed, taste and season very well with salt, pepper and nutmeg. Cover and allow to stand for a couple of hours (or even overnight) in the refrigerator to firm up.

4 To make the sauce, scrub the lemons under hot water to remove any wax. Thinly pare the rind (zest) using a potato peeler, avoiding the bitter white pith. Squeeze the juice from 1 lemon. Melt the butter in a small pan. Add the lemon rind and bay leaves. Heat gently for 2 minutes then turn off the heat and leave in a warm place to infuse for at least 1 hour (the longer the better).

5 Take large teaspoonfuls of the mixture and quickly roll into small balls – no need to be too neat. Place on a tray lined with a tea towel sprinkled with flour.

6 Reheat the butter and strain into another pan. Stir in the lemon juice and bring to the boil (it will splutter). Season with salt and pepper. Keep warm. Spoon a third of this sauce into a warmed shallow serving bowl.

7 Bring a large pan of salted water to the boil, drop in all the *gnocchi* at once and cook for 2–3 minutes, once the water returns to the boil. They are cooked when they float to the surface. Lift out with a slotted spoon, draining well and transfer to the warmed dish. Pour over the lemony butter. Serve with freshly grated Parmesan cheese.

Baked gnocchi with pancetta, parmesan and sage

Gnocchi alla romana con pancetta e salvia

There are many types of gnocchi *in Italy, and this one is very rich! It is my variation of* gnocchi alla romana – gnocchi *in the Roman way. The* gnocchi *are made from semolina flour (durum wheat flour), cooked until thick with milk, cheeses and sage.*

SERVES 4

1 litre/1¾ pints/4 cups milk
250g/9oz semolina (durum) flour
175g/6oz/2 cups freshly grated Parmesan
125g/4½oz/8 tablespoons butter
2 egg yolks
1 tablespoon Dijon mustard
2 tablespoons chopped fresh sage
3 tablespoons chopped fresh parsley
150g/5oz unsmoked pancetta, thinly sliced
a handful of fresh sage leaves
salt and freshly ground black pepper

1 Pour the milk into a saucepan and whisk in the semolina. Bring slowly to the boil, stirring all the time until it really thickens – about 10 minutes.
2 Beat in half the Parmesan, half the butter, the egg yolks, mustard, and herbs. Taste and season well. Spread the mixture on to a baking tray (sheet) lined with cling film (plastic wrap) to a depth of 1 cm/½ in. Cover with cling film (plastic wrap) and leave to cool and set, about 2 hours.
3 When set, cut into triangles or circles with a 3.5 cm /1½ in biscuit (cookie) cutter.

4 Butter an ovenproof dish well and scatter the trimmings over the base. Dot with butter, scatter over half the pancetta and sprinkle with a little Parmesan. Arrange the *gnocchi* shapes in a single layer over the trimmings. Dot with butter and scatter over the remaining pancetta and sage leaves. Sprinkle with the remaining Parmesan.
5 Bake in a preheated oven 230°C/ 450°F/Gas 8 for 20–25 minutes until golden and crusty and the bacon is crisp. Leave to stand for 5 minutes. Serve.

Saffron and Parmesan risotto

Risotto alla Milanese

This simple but extremely rich and delicious risotto is usually served with Ossobuco *(see page 116). Try to use saffron strands for this – they impart a fantastic aroma to the rice. It is traditional to make this risotto with beef marrow, but if you prefer, use butter instead.*

SERVES 6

50g/2oz beef marrow (from the shin bone)
50g/2oz/4 tablespoons butter
1 large onion, finely chopped
150ml/¼ pint/⅔ cup dry white wine
500g/1lb 2oz/2¼ cups Italian risotto rice (Arborio, Carnaroli)
1 sachet saffron threads
1.5 litres/2¾ pints/6¾ cups hot meat stock (broth) (see page 49)
75g/3oz/1 cup freshly grated Parmesan
salt and freshly ground black pepper

1 Melt the beef marrow slowly with half the butter in a large saucepan and add the onion. Cook gently for 10 minutes until soft and golden but not coloured. Pour in the wine and boil hard to reduce until almost disappeared.
2 Pour in the rice, stir for a few minutes to toast it, then add the saffron and stir until well coated with melted marrow and heated through.

3 Begin to add the stock (broth) a large ladleful at a time, stirring until each ladleful is absorbed into the rice. Continue in this way until the rice is tender and creamy, but the grains are still firm (this should take 15–20 minutes depending on the type of rice).
4 Taste and season well with salt and pepper and stir in the remaining butter and Parmesan. Cover and rest for a couple of minutes then serve straight away.

Beetroot risotto with grilled radicchio and Fontina

Risotto di barbabietole con radicchio e Fontina alla griglia [v]

This is an unusual and beautiful risotto stained with the pink colour of earthy beetroot, and topped with slightly bitter grilled radicchio. I had a risotto like this in Verona, topped with a melting layer of Fontina cheese, which I stirred into the risotto in long strings.

SERVES 4

three small heads of radicchio, halved

3 tablespoons olive oil

125g/4½oz/8 tablespoons butter

1 red onion, chopped

500g/1lb 2oz uncooked cooked beetroot, diced

500g/1lb 2oz/2½ cups risotto rice

2 tablespoons raspberry vinegar

about 1 litre/1¾ pints/4 cups hot vegetable stock (broth) (see page 49)

3 tablespoons chopped fresh parsley

300g/11oz Fontina cheese, thinly sliced

salt and freshly ground black pepper

1 Preheat the grill (broiler). Lay the radicchio halves cut-side up on a grill pan and brush with oil. Place under the grill (broiler) and grill (broil) for about 10–15 minutes until soft and beginning to colour. Remove from the grill (broiler) and set aside.

2 Heat half the butter and add the onion. Cook gently for 10 minutes until softening. Add the beetroot, and cook, stirring constantly over the heat for about 10 minutes until softening. Stir in the rice to coat it with the oil and vegetables. Cook for a couple of minutes to toast the grains a little.

3 Add the vinegar, stir and allow to evaporate. Begin to add the stock (broth) a large ladleful at a time, stirring until each ladleful is absorbed. Continue until the rice is tender and creamy, but the grains still firm and the beetroot is beginning to disintegrate (20 minutes depending on the type of rice). Stir in the remaining butter.

4 Taste and season well with salt and pepper and stir in the parsley. Ladle into 4 bowls and place a radicchio half on the top of each one. Cover with the Fontina, set on a baking tray (sheet) and grill (broil) for 5 minutes until the cheese is melted. Serve immediately.

Cuttlefish risotto

Risotto nero

ANNA DEL CONTE has painstakingly researched the food and cooking of northern Italy, and is an expert on the cooking of risotto and Italian rices.

SERVES 4–5

900g/2lbs cuttlefish, or 600g/1¼lbs
   cleaned weight
1 onion, finely chopped
2 cloves garlic, very finely chopped
3 tablespoons olive oil
300ml/10fl oz/1¼ cup dry white wine
1.5 litres/2¾ pints/6¾ cups vegetable or light
   fish stock (broth) (see page 49)
75g/3oz/5 tablespoons butter
450g/1lb/2¼ cups Italian risotto rice,
   preferably Vialone Nano
2 tablespoons brandy
2 tablespoons grated Parmesan
salt and freshly ground black pepper

This recipe from Venice uses cuttlefish, a favourite seafood of the Venetians. The cuttlefish ink is used too, not just to give a black 'designer' look to the risotto, but also – and most importantly – for the stronger fish flavour. Cuttlefish are often caught in British waters, mainly during the early spring and are available in good fishmongers. Local cuttlefish are usually large, about 450g/1lb each, and they are more suitable for slow cooking, as in this recipe, than for grilling (broiling) and frying. Instead of cuttlefish you could use squid, which are more easily available. They cook more quickly, and the flavour is similar to cuttlefish, although less strong. You can cook the cuttlefish in advance, even the day before, and keep it refrigerated. Heat before you add it to the rice. The rice used in Venice is Vialone Nano, a semifino variety available in good Italian food shops. However, the more common Arborio will do perfectly well. ADC

1 Wash the cuttlefish, and slice the body into thin short strips and the tentacles into morsels. If you are using them, keep the ink sacs separate and do not lose them!
2 Put the onion, garlic, oil and 1 teaspoon of salt in a heavy-based saucepan and cook gently until the onion is soft and translucent. Throw in the cuttlefish and sauté gently for 10 minutes or so, stirring frequently. Add half the wine and cover the pan. Now the cuttlefish must cook until tender on the lowest heat, which will take at least 45 minutes. Keep a watch on the pan. Stir every now and then and check that the cuttlefish is always cooking in some liquid. If necessary, add a little boiling water.
3 Heat the stock (broth) and keep it gently simmering all through the preparation of the risotto. In another large, heavy-based saucepan, heat half the butter until just sizzling and add the rice. 'Toast' the rice (as we say in Italian) over a lively heat for about 1–1½ minutes and then pour over the rest of the wine. Stir and cook for about 1 minute to reduce the alcohol content of the wine.

4 Now you begin to make the risotto proper by adding the simmering stock (broth) by the ladleful. Half-way through the cooking – Vialone Nano takes about 15 minutes to cook, Arborio a couple of minutes longer – scoop in the cuttlefish and all the juices. Squeeze in the ink from the sacs, or add the water with the ink sachets dissolved in it. Mix well and continue cooking until the rice is done.
5 A few minutes before you think the rice is cooked, stir in the brandy. Draw the pan off the heat and add the remaining butter, plenty of pepper and the Parmesan. Leave covered for a minute or two, then give the risotto a good stir and transfer to a warm serving dish. Risotto does not like waiting – serve it immediately.

TIP: Ask your fishmonger to clean your cuttlefish and to give you the little ink sac or sacs intact. You can buy cuttlefish ink already prepared in little sachets. For this recipe you would need 2 sachets of ink. Squeeze them into a cupful of hot water and pour a little water into the sachet to rinse out all the ink.

Tyrolean dumplings

Canederli Tirolesi

CLAUDIA RODEN has contributed this unusual northern Italian recipe for traditional bread dumplings – they are a staple in any household from this area of Italy, designed to take the edge off the appetite so that less meat would be eaten.

SERVES 6

about 1.5 litres/2¾ pints/6¾ cups light meat stock (broth) (see page 49)
150g/5oz *speck* or smoked raw ham in one piece
3 eggs
250ml/8fl oz/1 cup milk
250g/9oz/4½ cups stale white bread, crumbled
1 tablespoon chopped chives
2 tablespoons chopped parsley
pinch freshly grated nutmeg
about 200–225g/7–8oz/1⅓–1⅔ cups plain (all-purpose) flour
salt and freshly ground black pepper

These dumplings are also called knödel *in German-speaking Alto Adige. The use of bread is very important to the cuisine here, hence its use in the dumplings.* Speck *is a delicious salted and smoked pork, which is eaten for breakfast, as an appetiser and used in much of the cooking here. The* canederli *are served with melted butter or grated cheese or in a soup of delicate meat or chicken broth. They are very large and very filling and one or two are enough per person. As with all dumplings, the flour quantities are not exact – it is all done by feel – you may need more, you may need less, depending on the other ingredients. CR*

1 Put the stock (broth) into a large pan and bring to the boil then cover and turn down the heat. Cut the *speck* or ham into very small cubes. Beat the eggs with the milk, add the bread and the cubed *speck* or ham, chives, parsley, salt, pepper and the nutmeg.

2 Lightly mix in enough flour to make a consistency that will hold together, but is not too dry. (It is a good idea to test one at this stage, then you will know whether to add more flour to the dough – see cooking instructions below). Mix it well then, with wet hands, make balls a little larger than an egg and place on a tray.

3 When all the *canederli* are ready, lightly dust with flour and gently lower them into the simmering stock. Poach in the stock for 20 minutes or until they rise and float up to the surface. Lift them out with a slotted spoon and place in warmed bowls. Pour over the strained broth and serve.

Little rice oranges

Arancine di riso

ANNA TASCA LANZA explains how to make this national dish of Sicily, which is eaten as street food on the way to work, or just to fill a hole. They come in different shapes and with different fillings, but the classic version is round like a little orange, as shown here.

MAKES 8–12

FOR THE FILLING:

280g/10oz chopped meat, half beef and half pork

1 carrot, peeled and diced

1 celery stalk, diced

1 onion, finely chopped

2 tablespoons olive oil

450ml/16fl oz/2 cups thin tomato sauce

1 tablespoon *estratto* or sun-dried tomato paste

FOR THE RISOTTO:

1 small onion

15g/½oz/1 tablespoon butter

2 tablespoons olive oil

450g/1lb risotto rice (Arborio or Carnaroli)

1 litre/1¾ pints/4 cups water

2 stock (bouillon) cubes

4 threads or ¼ teaspoon powdered saffron

2 heaped tablespoons grated Parmesan

salt and freshly ground black pepper

FOR THE BATTER:

2 tablespoons plain (all-purpose) flour

120ml/4fl oz/½ cup water

2 eggs

pinch of salt

plenty of dried breadcrumbs

vegetable oil, for deep frying

tomato sauce, for serving (optional)

Arancine, or rice balls, are street snacks which are very popular with Sicilian families. We all make them. Saffron gives the traditional flavour and colour. It was only in medieval times that saffron spread through the cuisines of the Mediterranean countries, leaving indelible traces everywhere – in Spain with paella, *in France with* bouillabaisse, *and in Italy with* risotto alla Milanese, *to mention a few. Had it not grown wild in Sicily, I think there would not be so many uses for saffron in our kitchen. The only place in Italy where saffron is cultivated commercially is in the hills of the province of Aquila. It has been cultivated there since the fifteenth century, and is said to be the best in the world. ATL*

1 Make the filling one day ahead, so that it thickens and will be easier to use. Sauté the meat, carrot, celery, and onion in olive oil until browned. Add the tomato sauce and the tomato paste. Cook over low heat for about 30 minutes, or until the sauce is thick. Cool and refrigerate.

2 To make the risotto, sauté the onion in the butter and olive oil, add the rice and water, stir, and put the lid on. As soon as it comes to a boil, add the stock cubes and the saffron. It is most important that the risotto becomes golden with saffron. Stir again, and when it comes back to the boil, stir again, then turn off the heat and cover. Wait for 20 minutes, and the rice will be done. Add the Parmesan, salt, and pepper, stir and pour out on to a platter. Spread out and wait for it to cool.

3 Now make the batter – this is important because it is what prevents the *arancine* from falling apart when you deep-fry them. Mix the flour with the water in a large flat dish with high sides, until there are no lumps. Add the eggs, one at a time, and combine well, using a whisk. Stir in the salt. Prepare a platter with plenty of breadcrumbs. Put a bowl of cold water next to you, to wet your hands now and then – this will help the rice stick together.

4 To assemble the rice balls, wet your hands in the cold water and fill the palm of 1 hand with a tablespoonful of rice. Cup your hand and make a hole in the middle, pushing the rice to the same thickness all around. Fill the hole with 1 tablespoon of stuffing and close your hand, enclosing the meat sauce with the rice. Add more if you need to make the ball round. Keep the hand with which you are spreading the rice wet. The ball should be no bigger than a small orange.

5 As you make them, lay the *arancine* side by side in the batter, and when all are ready, coat them, one by one, compacting them with your hands. Coat them with the breadcrumbs, pat them thoroughly with your hands and put them on a tray.

6 Heat the vegetable oil in a very large frying pan. Drop in a little ball of batter coated with breadcrumbs to test the temperature. This will sizzle when the oil is hot enough. Slip in the *arancine* so they sit with the oil reaching three-quarters of the way up the ball. With a slotted spoon, sprinkle oil on top of the *arancine* turning one now and then to see if it is golden. Brown on the other side. Remove them and lay on absorbent paper. Eat warm with tomato sauce on the side, if you like.

Potato gnocchi

Gnocchi di patate [v]

CLAUDIO PECORARI's *gnocchi* are legendary. He is a chef originally from Trentino, but works internationally. He has the lightest touch, and has been making *gnocchi* since he was old enough to peer over the top of a kitchen table. Read the recipe before you start, and remember not to overwork the dough. Work as quickly as you can, and you will have *gnocchi* as light and airy as Claudio's. The potato used mustn't be a waxy variety, but dry and floury. *Gnocchi* are made all over northern Italy, particularly in Trentino.

SERVES 6

3 medium-sized floury baking potatoes, skin on
About 300–400g/11–14oz/2–2½ cups plain white (all-purpose) flour
2 eggs
freshly grated nutmeg
salt and freshly ground black pepper

This is my basic potato gnocchi *dough. The secret is not to add too much egg or flour to the potatoes – just enough to bind the mixture together, but still keep it light. You need pastry hands for* gnocchi *rather than bread dough hands! CP*

1 Put the unpeeled potatoes in a large pan and cover with cold water. Bring to the boil and simmer the potatoes until cooked. Leaving the peel on helps to retain the starch. Test with a skewer – they must be very tender. Put another large pan of salted water on to boil to be ready for cooking the *gnocchi*.
2 Drain and peel the potatoes while still hot and pass through a potato ricer, spreading the pile evenly on a clean work surface to a thickness of about 2.5cm/1in thick to preserve some of the warmth. Thinner than that, and it will cool too fast and became grainy, but any thicker and the potato will continue to cook and become gluey. Sprinkle about half of the flour (you may not need it all) evenly over the surface of the to prevent the formation of dried bits, which will show in the potato dough, and season.
3 When the dough is just tepid, break the eggs in and start working the mixture with your fingers, raising it from the bottom to top. Continue to do so until the dough starts to form into large lumps. If it's too wet add some more flour (you may not need it all). Keep mixing and gently folding the mixture until is smooth, roll it on the side.
4 Roll part of the dough into a finger-thick sausage, and cut into bite size pieces. As soon you have a couple of portions, toss them in the boiling water. Do not stir, as the *gnocchi* will rise to the surface by themselves. To help them rise, tap the sides of the pot with a wooden spoon.
5 Allow them to cook for another approximately 2 minutes and scoop them out of the water with a slotted spoon on to a plate. Continue with the rest of the dough until all are cooked. Serve hot with accompanied by anything from plain butter to rich gamey ragouts or *Gulasch* (see page 117).

5

Fish
and Shellfish

'Harlot's' tuna in a parcel

Tuna puttanesca 'in cartoccio'

VALENTINA HARRIS teaches us a method of steaming fish in its own juices and some additional flavourings. This technique is particularly good for tuna, as it can be rather dry if overcooked.

In this recipe, the tuna is smothered in an assertive, passionate and rough and ready sauce from southern Italy. Legend has it that this was a sauce quickly rustled up between clients! It goes really well with the meaty flesh of the tuna, which is kept moist by cooking in paper or 'in cartoccio'. Tuna is cut much thinner in the south of Italy than it is in England, for example, where retaining its moisture is more important. VH

SERVES 4

1 clove garlic, crushed
8 tablespoons extra virgin olive oil
3 anchovy fillets (either salted or in canned in oil, rinsed and dried)
1 tablespoon salted capers, rinsed, dried and chopped
200g/7oz/scant 1 cup canned chopped Italian tomatoes
4 x 150g/5oz slices fresh tuna
2 tablespoons plain white (all-purpose) flour
4 tablespoons dry white wine
large pinch dried oregano
handful of stoned black olives
salt and freshly ground black pepper
boiled new potatoes, olive oil, flat-leaf parsley and grated lemon rind (zest), to serve

1 Preheat the oven to 180°C/350°F/Gas 5. Fry the garlic in half the oil together with the anchovy until the anchovy dissolves. Add the capers, tomatoes and seasoning and stir. Simmer for a few minutes and then take off the heat.

2 Heat the rest of the oil and coat the tuna steaks lightly in flour. Fry the tuna steaks briefly on each side for 2 minutes, then add the wine to the pan and boil off for another minute.

3 Transfer each steak on to a big square of baking parchment. Stir the oregano and olives into the sauce and cover the steaks evenly with the sauce. Close the paper around the tuna and sauce, loose enough to fill it with steam but secure enough not to let the sauce or the tuna seep out.

4 Bake in the oven for 15 minutes, and serve with boiled new potatoes sprinkled with olive oil and chopped flat-leaf parsley with a little grated lemon rind (zest) .

Stewed squid with tomato and peas

Calamari e piselli alla livornese

ALVARO MACCIONE is an inspirational teacher and restaurateur, whose knowledge of all things Tuscan is overwhelming! Here he shows us how to deal with squid, a favourite with all Italians.

SERVES 4–6

1½ tablespoons finely chopped onion

3 tablespoons olive oil

1–2 cloves garlic, peeled and
    finely chopped

1 tablespoon finely chopped parsley

175g/6oz/¾ cup canned Italian tomatoes
    coarsely chopped with their juice

1kg/2¼ lbs smallest possible squid, cleaned
    by the fishmonger

1kg/2¼ lbs fresh peas or 300g/11oz frozen
    peas, thawed

salt and freshly ground black pepper

My father decreed that we could not eat any fish that did not look like a fish, so I had to eat squid in secret when I was away from home. I would eat this at my aunt Adrianna's house when peas were in season. I used to pick them for her from her garden – they were so sweet and tender that I always ate some of them straight out of the pod while I was picking! This stewed squid can be prepared entirely ahead of time and refrigerated for up to two days, if you like. Warm up slowly just before serving. AM

1 Put the onion in a casserole with the olive oil and sauté over a medium heat until it begins to turn pale gold. Add the garlic and sauté until it colours lightly but does not brown. Add the parsley, stir once or twice, then add the tomatoes. Cook at a gentle simmer for 10 minutes.

2 Slice the squid tubes into rings about 18–25 mm/¾ –1in wide. Divide the tentacle cluster into two parts. Add all the squid to the casserole then add the salt and pepper, stir, cover and cook at a gentle simmer for 30 minutes.

3 If you are using fresh peas add them to the casserole at this point. Cover and continue cooking until the squid is tender, about another 20 minutes. (Cooking times, however, vary considerably, depending on the size and toughness of the squid, so test from time to time with a fork.) When the squid is easily pierced, it is done. If you are using thawed frozen peas add them to the casserole when the squid is practically done, as they need only a few minutes cooking. Check the seasoning. Serve hot.

Venetian scampi sautéed with breadcrumbs and wine

Scampi alla buzara

FULVIA SESANI's recipe from her native Veneto makes the most of an expensive ingredient. It shows how the addition of breadcrumbs can make the sauce go further – a common technique used throughout Italy.

SERVES 6–8

120ml/4fl oz/½ cup extra virgin olive oil
5 cloves garlic
450g/1lb Dublin Bay prawns
    (scampi), shelled
250ml/8fl oz/1 cup dry white wine
450ml/¾ pint/2 cups chicken stock (broth)
    (see page 49)
1 teaspoon hot paprika
8 tablespoons stale breadcrumbs
2 tablespoons parsley, finely chopped
sea salt
croûtons, to serve

'Buzara' means 'to cheat' in Venetian dialect. This dish is called 'cheat's scampi' because it requires only a small quantity of Dublin Bay prawns (scampi), which are always very expensive, as well as lots of sauce. It comes from the Istrian coast, which was once under Venetian domination and is full of fishermen, who are a very parsimonious lot! FS

1 In a large sauté pan heat the oil, add the garlic and cook for a few minutes. Remove the garlic before it burns, and discard, retaining the oil.
2 Add the prawns (scampi) and sauté briefly to coat in the garlic-flavoured olive oil.
3 Add the wine a little at the time, so it evaporates between each addition. Pour in the stock (broth), stir in the paprika and breadcrumbs, raise the heat and bring to the boil. Turn down the heat and simmer for 20 minutes. Add the parsley and salt to taste. Serve with croûtons.

Lobster sauce for pasta

Spaghetti con salsa di aragostini

This sauce is only made from the tiny sweet lobsters found on the south-west coast of Sicily near Agrigento and Selinunte. I first tasted it in Ristorante da Vittorio in Porto Palo, gazing out over the glittering sea towards Tunisia – I was in heaven! If you can't find small lobsters, the equivalent weight in Dublin Bay prawns (scampi) or even lobster tails would do.

SERVES 6

3 small live lobsters or lobster tails, weighing about 400g/14oz each
3 tablespoons olive oil
2–3 cloves garlic, chopped
large pinch crushed red chilli
120ml/4fl oz/½ cup dry white wine
2 tablespoons chopped fresh parsley
salt and freshly ground black pepper
625g/1lb 6oz dried spaghetti, freshly boiled

1 Bring a pan of salted water to the boil and drop in one lobster. Simmer for 12 minutes, cool and remove the flesh.
2 Split the other two lobsters in half, remove the stomach sac, then chop both into large pieces, including the legs and the head.

3 Heat the oil in a sauté pan, add the garlic and chilli, and the chopped lobster. Sauté for a couple of minutes, then add the wine. Bring to the boil, add the boiled lobster and stir in the parsley. Simmer for 1 minute, then season.
4 Toss with freshly boiled spaghetti and eat the meat from the shells with your fingers.

Baked swordfish rolls

Involtini di pesce spada

These little rolls are a speciality of the Trattoria Stella in Palermo's old back streets – it is situated in a crumbling courtyard, covered in plumbago and jasmine, and is a haven from the buzz of Vespas, Piaggios and other traffic. There are all sorts of fillings for these little skewered rolls. A piccante cheese goes very well in the filling, and the breadcrumb coating adds a crunchiness. These are delicious served alongside Sarde alla beccaficu, or Sardines to look like fig-peckers (see page 34) as part of a main course.

SERVES 4

8 slices or 750g/1lb 10oz fresh swordfish, sliced 5mm/¼in thick

1 clove garlic, crushed

1 tablespoon chopped fresh sage

2 dried bay leaves, crumbled

1 tablespoon chopped fresh rosemary

1 teaspoon dried chilli flakes

1 whole mozzarella, grated

2 tablespoons olive oil

6 slices bread, crusts removed, made into breadcrumbs

2 tablespoons freshly grated pecorino (romano) or Parmesan

1 teaspoon dried oregano

2 eggs, beaten

16 fresh bay leaves

2 lemons, cut into wedges

4 small red onions, cut into wedges

salt and freshly ground black pepper

1 Soak some bamboo or wooden skewers in cold water for at least 20 minutes.

2 Using a wooden rolling pin, bat out each piece of swordfish between sheets of cling film (plastic wrap) until thin.

3 Mix the garlic with the herbs, chilli and mozzarella. Spread this evenly over the slices, season with salt and pepper.

4 Roll up each slice tightly and secure with a cocktail stick. Roll in a little olive oil to coat, then refrigerate for at 1 hour.

5 Mix the fresh breadcrumbs with the cheese and oregano. Dip each roll in the egg, then the breadcrumb mixture to coat. Thread on to double bamboo skewers alternating with the bay leaves, lemon wedges and onion wedges.

6 Drizzle with a little olive oil, and grill or barbecue for 2–3 minutes on each side until cooked.

A whole fish baked in a salt crust

Pesce al sale

The beauty of this dish is in its simplicity. Whole sea trout, salmon, sea bass and even red snapper all work well treated in this way, which makes the flesh moist, the flavour intense and not salty. Salt is produced in Sicily by ancient methods of evaporation, and is imported to the mainland – I love it prepared in this way and it is ideal for this cooking method. I always try and bring some back with me when I visit Italy.

SERVES 8

2 x 2kg/4½lb whole fish, unscaled
   and ungutted
3–4 fronds of dill or wild fennel
2 egg whites
approx. 2kg/4½lbs sea salt, depending on
   size of dish

1 Choose two large oval or rectangular baking dishes into which your fish will fit very comfortably without touching the edges. Lightly wipe out with oil.
2 Lightly beat the egg whites with 6 tablespoons water and mix with the sea salt – do it with your hands, like rubbing in the fat when making pastry.
3 Cover the bases of the dishes with a 2.5 cm /1in layer of sea salt. Lay the fish on top, cover with dill fronds and cover thickly with the remaining moist salt (the scales will protect the fish from the salt and as the fish is ungutted, it retains its moisture during cooking).
4 Bake at 190ºC/375ºF/Gas 5 for about 1 hour. Remove from the oven and rest it for 10 minutes. Carry ceremoniously to the table and crack the crust open (you may need a hammer for this!). The herbs and skin may come away with the salt crust. Serve as quickly as possible.

Stuffed mussels in the Pistoia style

Muscoli ripieni alla Pistoiese

ALVARO MACCIONE's recipe for mussels seems a little labour-intensive, but is an interesting technique, and well worthwhile – the flavour is amazing. This is a substantial dish, as with most Tuscan food!

The Tuscan coastline is the longest in Italy and yet people do not recognize that there are many fish dishes here – in fact it has the widest range of fish dishes in Italy. I call these mussels muscoli *because, in Tuscany, we have learnt this from the English! In the rest of Italy, mussels are always known as* cozze. *Pistoia is the nearest town within Tuscany to Bologna, hence the rich filling! AM*

SERVES 4

1.2kg/2½ lbs live mussels, as large as
    you can find
2 cloves garlic, chopped
1 tablespoon chopped fresh parsley

FOR THE STUFFING:
150g/5oz fresh Italian *salsicce*
    (Italian sausage)
50g/2oz mortadella
soft part of 1 bread roll
1 clove garlic, chopped
1 teaspoon chopped fresh parsley
1 egg, beaten
salt and freshly ground black pepper

FOR THE SAUCE:
3 tablespoons olive oil
1 onion, chopped
1 teaspoon chopped fresh parsley
500g/1lb 2oz fresh, ripe tomatoes, skinned,
    de-seeded and puréed
salt and freshly ground black pepper

1 Preheat the oven to 180°C/350°F/Gas 4. Scrub and de-beard the mussels and wash them carefully in several changes of water. Discard any that do not close when sharply tapped.
2 Put the mussels into a saucepan over a medium heat with the garlic and parsley. Shake the pan from time to time and remove the mussels as they open up. Discard any that do not open.
3 In the meantime, mince (grind) the sausage and the mortadella together in the food processor. Soak the bread in water and then squeeze it. Mix these ingredients together with the garlic, parsley and egg. Season with salt and a pinch of pepper.
4 Put the oil in a casserole and sauté the onion with the parsley for a few minutes. Add the tomatoes, salt and pinch of pepper and simmer for about 20 minutes. Then transfer to an oiled ovenproof dish.
5 Fill the mussels with the stuffing, tie up each shell with white cook's string so that they do not open during cooking, and arrange them on the tomato sauce. Bake for 20 minutes, remove the cook's string and serve.

Braised sea bass with fennel and green olives

Branzino brasato al forno con finocchio e olive verde

The delicate but meaty flesh of the sea bass goes so well with braised fennel, wine and olives. This is a classic dish served in many Mediterranean restaurants. The whole fish is braised in a steamy bed of sliced fennel and plump green olives. Baking a whole fish this way keeps the flesh moist – the skin holds in the all the juices. Take the fish off the bed of vegetables, lift the skin away and the cooked flesh should pull away from the bone. Fish cooked on the bone always has more flavour than plain filleted fish. You will rarely see headless fish in an Italian fish-market.

SERVES 4

1.2kg/2½ lb sea bass or sea bream, scaled
  and gutted
a few sprigs fresh wild fennel or fennel herb
2 large fennel bulbs
150ml/5fl oz/⅔ cup good olive oil
juice of 1 lemon
1 tablespoon dried oregano
3 tablespoons chopped fresh parsley
12 large green olives, stoned
150ml/¼ pint/⅔ cup dry white wine
salt and freshly ground black pepper

1 Preheat the oven to 220°C/425°F/Gas 7. Wash the fish inside and out, pat dry. Fill the cavity with wild fennel.
2 Cut the fennel bulbs in half lengthways, cut out the core and slice thickly. Blanch in boiling salted water for 5 minutes. Drain.
3 Whisk the oil, lemon juice, herbs, salt and pepper together in a medium bowl and stir in the fennel and olives to coat. Tip this mixture into a shallow oval dish that will take the fish as well. Lay the fish on top of the fennel and pour over any remaining liquid, then the wine.
4 Bake in the oven for 30 minutes. Spoon the juices over the fish and stir the fennel around and leave in the oven. Turn off the oven, close the door and leave for 5 minutes for the fish to 'set'. Serve immediately or leave to cool and serve at room temperature.

Carpaccio of fresh tuna with fresh salmoriglio

Carpaccio di tonno con salmoriglio fresco

For this dish the tuna must be paper thin or the effect is ruined. Carpaccio (made with beef) was originally created by Giuseppe Cipriani at Harry's Bar in Venice in the 1950s and was named after the Renaissance painter Carpaccio who used red and white in his palette.

SERVES 4–6

250g/9oz piece of tuna loin
juice of 3 lemons
150ml/¼ pint/⅔ cup extra virgin olive oil
1 clove garlic, finely chopped
1 tablespoon rinsed salted capers, chopped
2 teaspoons dried oregano
salt and freshly ground black pepper
125g/4½oz wild or cultivated rocket (arugula)
   and shaved Parmesan, to serve

1 Trim the tuna of any membrane or gristle. Wrap tightly in cling film (plastic wrap) and place in the freezer for about 1 hour until just frozen and firm but not rock solid.

2 Meanwhile, whisk the lemon juice, olive oil, garlic, capers, oregano, salt and pepper together until thick and well emulsified.

3 Unwrap the tuna, slice thinly with a thin-bladed, very sharp knife. Arrange the slices over four large dinner plates. Spoon the dressing over the tuna. Top with a tangle of rocket (arugula) leaves and scatter with shaved Parmesan.

Red mullet with creamy mint sauce

Triglie con salsa fredda di menta

This is a very ancient Arab recipe still made in the Palermo area today. The use of mint and breadcrumbs is typically Palerman. I buy my fish from either the Capo market or the Vucciria market once a week in Palermo.

SERVES 6

50g/2oz/1 cup day old stale breadcrumbs
3 tablespoons white wine vinegar
3 tablespoons chopped fresh mint
3 tablespoons chopped fresh parsley
1 tablespoon salted capers, rinsed
1 egg, beaten
2 teaspoons sugar
2 teaspoons anchovy paste
150ml/¼ pint/⅔ cup light fruity olive oil
900g/2lbs small red mullet, cleaned
   and scaled
seasoned flour (see method)
lemon wedges, to serve

1 Moisten the breadcrumbs with 2 tablespoons of the vinegar and a little water. Let it stand for a couple of minutes then gently squeeze out the moisture.

2 Put the breadcrumbs, mint, parsley, capers, egg, sugar and anchovy into a food processor. Blend until smooth.

3 With the machine running, gradually add the oil in a steady stream as if making mayonnaise. Taste and season, add the remaining vinegar if necessary. The sauce should be pale green and slightly sweet-and-sour. It is quite difficult to get the correct balance – keep tasting. Transfer to a bowl and cover.

4 Lightly coat the fish in flour and fry for about 3 minutes until golden on each side. Arrange on a platter with lemon wedges and serve the sauce in a bowl. Serve at room temperature.

Purée of salt cod

Baccalà mantecato

FRANCESCO ZANCHETTA is a gifted chef with a talent for explaining his cooking methods. This dish and the method is essential to any book covering the cuisine of Italy, as salt cod is used throughout the country, particularly in the north. It is said to have been brought originally as trade by the Vikings and later the Normans but has now become part of Italian culture.

SERVES 8

500g/1lb 2oz salt cod
500ml/18fl oz/2¼ cups milk
1 clove garlic, finely chopped
2 tablespoons chopped parsley
150ml/5fl oz/⅔ cup mild olive oil
freshly ground black pepper

This is one of the best recipes ever for cooking salt cod. I remember trying it for the first time at Harry's Bar in Venice. Heaven! Luckily, I was working there, so I got to learn how to prepare it. This recipe is slightly different from the original, as the kind of dried cod found outside Italy is different from the one used there. FZ

1 Soak the salt cod in cold water for 24 hours, changing the water at least 4 times. Taste a little piece of cod before you start working on it, to make sure that it is not very salty. If it is, soak it for longer.
2 Once soaked, the fish will be soft and easy to clean. Remove all the skin and bones, and break into thin strips following the fibre of the flesh. It is important not to cut it with a knife, or it will not bind when beaten.
3 Place in a large saucepan, add the milk and enough water to cover it completely. Boil for half an hour, taking care that the milk doesn't boil over. Drain, and pour into a mixer bowl, (a powerful mixer with a strong whisk is best, but a hand-held mixer can be used) and beat at high speed, for a minute or so, until the fish is all shredded and starting to stick. At this point add the garlic and parsley, and very slowly the olive oil, as if making a mayonnaise.
4 When all the oil has been absorbed, transfer to a dish and serve. It is best served on grilled polenta, but it can be served as a pâté on *crostini*.

6

Poultry
and Game

Duck with Valesana sauce

Anitra con salsa all Valesana

FULVIA SESANI's recipe for this unusual sweet and sour sauce clearly shows the Italian predilection for the contrast of sweet and savoury together – especially with game. There is a growing trend to revive medieval or Renaissance recipes in Italy, and this dish demonstrates how popular the use of spices and fruits were to those cuisines, and still are today, particularly in the Veneto region.

SERVES 4

2 wild duck or mallards
1 lemon, halved
2 bay leaves
50g/2oz/4 tablespoons butter, softened
salt and freshly ground black pepper

FOR THE SAUCE:
3 tablespoons unsalted (sweet) butter
2 tablespoons extra virgin olive oil
1 small onion, finely chopped
100g/4oz/½ cup salted anchovies, soaked, rinsed and boned
75g/3oz/½ cup sultanas (golden raisins), soaked in warm water for 2 hours
1 large dessert apple, peeled and finely chopped
50g/2oz/½ cup pine nuts
75g/3oz/½ cup sugar
120ml/4fl oz/½ cup white wine vinegar
120ml/4fl oz/½ cup dry white wine
1 teaspoon Dijon mustard
salt and freshly ground black pepper

The ingredients for this sauce recall the history of Venice, its trade with Byzantium and its eastern conquests. In the winter the marshlands of the Venetian lagoon are full of migratory birds, especially the wild duck known as 'osele', Venetian dialect for uccelli or 'birds'. In season, there are always lots of enthusiastic hunters who shoot them from their botti or barrels – duck-hides half-hidden in the water. Hemingway adored this type of hunting, and shot many ducks during his stays on the island of Torcello. It provides an extraordinary variety of wild fowl for our tables around Christmas time. Wild duck flesh has a strong and pungent flavour, which needs just this 'Valesana sauce' to mellow it.

In the days of the 'Serenissima' (Venetian Republic), the Doge used to give 'osele' as Christmas presents to the members of the Grand Council. Later, when it was no longer possible to obtain enough wild fowl for all members, gold and silver coins were minted with the head of the Doge, as substitutes. This custom lasted until the fall of the Republic, and now these replacement 'osele' are very rare and highly prized by collectors. FS

1 Preheat the oven to 200°C/400°F/Gas 6. Rinse the birds inside and out and pat dry with kitchen paper. Halve the lemon and rub the cut side all over the outside of the birds. Place each lemon half inside the cavities of the birds. Tuck a bay leaf inside with the lemon and season.

2 Spread the softened butter all over the breasts and legs of the birds and set them on a rack in a roasting tin (pan). Roast in the oven for 40 minutes.

3 Meanwhile, make the sauce. Heat a medium frying pan and add the butter and oil. When melted, add the onion and fry for 5 minutes. Add the anchovies and stir over a low heat until they melt.

4 Add the drained sultanas, then the chopped apple, the pine nuts and the sugar. Mix, gradually adding the vinegar and the wine a little at the time. Simmer over a low heat slowly for about 20 minutes, until the mixture has reduced by one third. Remove the pan from the heat, let it cool slightly, and stir in the mustard, taste and season. Transfer to a glass serving dish (serve warm or at room temperature).

5 Remove the ducks from the oven when ready, cover and leave to rest in a warm place for 10–15 minutes. This will make the birds more tender and juicy. Serve the ducks with the Valesana sauce.

GIULIANO BUGIALLI

Stuffed squab braised in wild mushroom sauce

Piccione ripieni in umido

GIULIANO BUGIALLI presents this autumnal recipe that makes the most out of the technique of braising squab with wild mushrooms, popular in the wooded areas of northern Italy. Squab in Britain are farmed birds, usually under seven months old, and in Italy they are farmed or wood pigeons. The meat is intense and should be cooked either very quickly over hot coals or stewed for a long time.

SERVES 8

4 squabs
1 small carrot, scraped
1 small celery stalk
1 medium-sized red onion, peeled
2 sage leaves, fresh
50g/2oz dried porcini (Boletus
  edulis) mushrooms
50ml/2fl oz/¼ cup olive oil
1 tablespoon unsalted (sweet) butter
120ml/4fl oz/½ cup dry red wine
250ml/8fl oz/1 cup canned Italian
  tomatoes, drained
2 tablespoons tomato purée (paste)
250ml/8fl oz/1 cup hot home-made chicken
  stock (broth) (see page 49)
900g/2lbs boiling potatoes (not new potatoes)
salt and freshly ground black pepper
sea salt, to serve
a few sprigs of celery leaves, to serve

FOR THE STUFFING:

2 fresh Italian sausages, without fennel seeds,
  or 175g/6oz minced (ground) pork
2 slices white bread, crusts removed
100g/4oz minced (ground) veal
salt and freshly ground black pepper

Squab is not an unusual main dish in Italy, and its flavoursome meat is also used for stuffing pasta and to flavour some sauces. In the following preparation, cooking it in red wine with dried porcini mushrooms brings out the intense flavour of the dark-fleshed squab. This is one of the few dishes in which riced or sieved potatoes are treated like polenta, as a part of the dish, to catch the rich sauce and stuffing. GB

1 Clean and wash the squabs well. Then pat them dry with paper towels. Remove any extra fat from the cavities.
2 To prepare the stuffing, remove the skin from the sausages and put the meat in a crockery or glass bowl. Soak the bread in a bowl of cold water for 2 minutes, then squeeze the water out of the bread and add the bread to the bowl with the sausage meat. Add the veal and salt and pepper to the bowl and mix very well with a wooden spoon. Stuff the cavity of each squab with one quarter of the mixture. Use a needle and thread to sew up the cavity of each squab. Truss the birds by tying down the wings and legs with string.
3 Finely chop the carrot, celery, onion, and sage together on a board. Soak the mushrooms in 450ml/¾ pint/2 cups of lukewarm water for ½ hour.
4 Heat the oil and butter in a casserole over medium heat and, when the butter is completely melted, add the chopped ingredients. Sauté for 5 minutes. Then add the squabs and sauté for 5 minutes, or until they are golden brown all over. Add the wine and let it evaporate over low heat (about 15 minutes).
5 Meanwhile, place a large pot with 2 litres/3½ pints/8 cups of cold water over a high heat.
6 Pass the tomatoes through a food mill, using the disc with the small holes, into a

small bowl and combine them with the tomato purée (paste). Add this mixture to the casserole and cook for 5 minutes.
7 Drain the soaked mushrooms, saving the water for later use. Be sure no earth or grit remains attached to the mushrooms, then add them to the casserole. Taste for salt and pepper and cook, covered, until the squabs are tender (about 25 minutes), adding hot stock (broth) as needed. As soon as the mushrooms are added to the casserole, pass the mushroom soaking water through a piece of heavy cheesecloth or several layers of paper towelling to strain out all the remaining grit.
8 When the water begins to boil, add the strained mushroom water and coarse-grained salt. Peel the potatoes and put them into the boiling water. Boil until the potatoes are cooked, but still firm (20 to 30 minutes, depending on the size of the potatoes). The potatoes and the squabs should be ready at the same time.
9 Quickly pass the potatoes through a potato ricer onto a large warm serving platter and pour the sauce in which the squabs have cooked all over the layer of riced potatoes.
10 Untie the squabs and arrange them in the centre of the platter over the potatoes. You will have to halve them to serve. Arrange the sprigs of celery leaves in the middle and serve immediately.

Wild boar chops in sweet and sour sauce

Costolette di cinghiale in agro dolce

FRANCO TARUSCHIO was born in Le Marche, a part of Italy that is rich in game. This unusual recipe for wild boar looks back to cooking in the days of the Renaissance and medieval Italy, involving sweet and sour flavours and chocolate. Try it with pork chops if wild boar is not available – it is incredible.

SERVES 4

4 wild boar chops (you can use pork chops
   instead, but they will not have that
   gamey flavour)
a little olive oil
1 tablespoon finely chopped candied citron or
   lemon peel
25g/1oz/¼ cup pine kernels
salt and freshly ground black pepper

FOR THE SAUCE:
8 tablespoons sugar
8 fresh or 4 dried bay leaves
450ml/16fl oz/2 cups red wine vinegar
175g/6oz/1 cup sultanas (golden raisins)
175g/6oz bitter (unsweetened) chocolate,
   chopped into small pieces
pinch of freshly grated nutmeg
175g/6oz prunes (pruneaux d'Agen are best)

Our restaurant, The Walnut Tree, is deep in the countryside in Wales. Through living in the country our chefs learn to respect the meat they handle. They have seen the animals in the fields around us, heard the farmers talking about nights spent out in the sheep sheds or fields in the freezing cold, bringing lambs into the world. We encourage our chefs to go to the farms so that they can develop more feeling and understanding for the product. The chefs have to realize that meat does not just arrive portion-controlled, wrapped in plastic. Wild boar is one of these – it roams wild in Italy and is much prized by the hunters. In Britain wild boar is farmed, deriving from Polish stock, and is widely available from good butchers. The meat is full of flavour and the fat when cooked crisply is delicious. We often served this at the restaurant. FT

1 To make the sauce, put the sugar, bay leaves and vinegar in a pan over a low heat and stir until the sugar is dissolved. Boil rapidly for 2–3 minutes to reduce the sauce to a light syrup. Add the sultanas (golden raisins), bitter (unsweetened) chocolate and nutmeg. Stir the sauce gently until the chocolate has melted. Stone the prunes and add. Keep warm.

2 Season the chops with salt and pepper and either grill (broil) or fry them in a little olive oil for about 4 minutes on each side depending on the thickness, until they are just cooked through. Leave the chops to rest in a warm place for 5 minutes.

3 To serve, pour the sauce over the chops and sprinkle the candied citron cubes and pine kernels over the top.

Turkey rolls with broad (fava) beans

Involtini di tacchino con fave

VALENTINA HARRIS demonstrates how to make escalopes with turkey meat and rolls them around a fresh bean and pecorino (romano) purée. The rolls are secured with blanched spring onions (scallions), but you could use cocktail sticks instead.

SERVES 4

600g/1lb 5oz fresh broad (fava)
   beans, podded
6 spring onions (scallions)
7 tablespoons extra virgin olive oil
3 sprigs fresh marjoram
4 tablespoons dry white wine
2 tablespoons grated fresh strong
   pecorino (romano)
freshly grated nutmeg
8 turkey escalopes or steaks
salt and freshly ground black pepper

With good, kindly raised veal more and more difficult to come by, turkey escalopes make a good substitute and are very popular in Italy. Turkey is eaten all over Italy, introduced from America. Broad (fava) beans freshly popped out of their skins are a beautiful green colour and coupled with ripe pecorino (romano) cheese, offer a taste of spring. VH

1 First peel the beans. Bring a pot of water to the boil and add the beans. Boil for 1 minute, drain then plunge into cold water and slip off their skins.

2 Chop 2 spring onions (scallions) and fry them with 4 tablespoons of olive oil and the marjoram. Add the broad (fava) beans and cook stir to coat them in the onion mixture, then add salt. Pour in the wine, cover and simmer for 20 minutes.

3 Divide the broad (fava) beans in half. Process half with the cheese and season well with nutmeg, salt and pepper.

4 Meanwhile, flatten the turkey into thin pieces between sheets of cling film (plastic wrap), using a rolling pin. Trim neatly. Fill the escalopes with the bean purée and, rolling the meat up around the filling.

5 Blanch the remaining spring onions (scallions) in boiling water for 2 minutes, cool and then cut them in half and use them to tie up the *involtini*, or, the little turkey rolls.

6 Heat the remaining oil in a wide frying-pan (skillet) and add any remaining spring onions (scallions) which you have chopped. Seal the tied *involtini* in the hot oil, then add the remaining whole beans and any remaining bean purée. Add a little water to keep moist, and cover. Simmer on a gentle heat for 20 minutes before serving with mashed potatoes.

Lemon chilli chicken

Pollo al limone e peperoncini

Chicken marinated in lemon juice becomes wonderfully tender – especially when marinated in sun-ripened fruits, young succulent garlic and fiery chilli flakes. This is a standard for my cookery classes at Villa Ravidà in Sicily. We let the chicken marinate all day, then light the big outdoor barbecue and grill the chicken over an olive wood and charcoal braise. So much is cooked outside on the barbecue during the summer months – it's far too hot to stay indoors.

SERVES 4

1 x 1.75kg/3½lb free-range chicken
4 really ripe juicy lemons
8 whole cloves garlic
1 small red chilli, seeded and chopped
2 tablespoons orange blossom honey
4 tablespoons chopped fresh parsley
salt and freshly ground black pepper

1 Using a sharp knife and kitchen scissors, cut the chicken into 8 joints. Place in a shallow ovenproof dish.
2 Squeeze the juice from the lemons and pour into a small bowl. Reserve the halves.
3 Skin and crush two of the garlic cloves, adding them to the lemon juice with the chilli and honey. Stir well, pour over the chicken and tuck the lemon halves around. Cover and leave to marinate for at least 2 hours or overnight, turning once.

4 Remove the lemon halves and discard. Turn the chicken skin side up, scatter over the remaining whole garlic cloves and roast in a preheated oven at 200°C/400°F/Gas 6 for 45 minutes, or until golden brown and tender. Or barbecue, turning frequently and basting with the lemon marinade. Stir in or scatter with the parsley, taste and season.

Devilled quails

Quaglie alla diavola

Quails prepared in this way are both easy to eat and easy to cook. They are 'spatchcocked', which means they are split open and flattened, marinated, skewered and then grilled over hot coals. The best way to eat these is with the fingers! Chickens and squabs can be cooked in the same manner. We cook these in Tuscany on a typical wood and ash braise on the brick hearth under a vast chimney in the kitchen – 'alla brace'. To make the braise, a fire is lit, and when the wood has turned to glowing red ashes, they are spread out in an even layer and left until white on top. A low iron grill on legs is placed over this braise and the spatchcocked birds are cooked on top. The smell is wonderful as they sizzle over the coals!

SERVES 4

8 quails
250ml/8fl oz/1 cup olive oil
juice of 1 lemon
2 cloves garlic, crushed
1 teaspoon hot chilli flakes
salt and freshly ground black pepper
lemon wedges, to serve

1 Take each quail and turn breast side down. You will see the backbone underneath the skin on the base, finishing with the parson's nose. Take a pair of kitchen scissors and cut along one side of the backbone. Cut along the other side and you will have removed the backbone.
2 Turn the birds over, breast side uppermost and open out. Press down hard on the breast bone until you hear a crack and the bird flattens out.
3 Mix the olive oil with the juice of the lemon, and the crushed garlic, adding a good pinch of salt and lots of ground pepper and chilli flakes. Pour this into a shallow dish that will take all the quail. Add the quail and turn in the marinade to coat. Cover and leave to marinate in the refrigerator for at least an hour.

4 Meanwhile soak some bamboo skewers in cold water for at least 20 minutes. Remove the birds from the refrigerator and marinade, and skewer them each with two skewers, pushing each skewer in diagonally from drumstick to wing bone through the breast. Each bird should now lie flat.
5 Grill or barbecue, with the skin side close to the heat for 12–15 minutes until cooked through and blackened but not burnt, turning twice. Baste with the marinade from time to time. Serve piping hot with lemon wedges. The birds are said to look like the shape of the devil's face, the charring is the colour of the devil and the chilli makes it hotter than hell!

Hare sauce for wide noodles

Pappardelle alla lepre

This really rich, wintry sauce has origins in Tuscany and, if hares are available, we try to make it every year at Fattoria Montellucci. They are not the nicest of things to prepare – quite bloody, but the resultant slow-cooked sauce is fabulous. Use rabbit for a much lighter sauce. Tuscans are not famed for making their own pasta, but they will make it specially for this dish – hare is really prized here. You will see this on many menus in local restaurants, but nothing beats making it at home.

SERVES 4

1 hare, skinned and jointed
3 tablespoons olive oil
4 tablespoons butter
1 medium onion, finely diced
1 medium carrot, finely diced
1 stick celery, finely diced
2 cloves garlic, chopped
75g/3oz unsmoked pancetta, or bacon, diced
2 tablespoons plain (all-purpose) flour
300ml / ½ pint/1¼ cups dry red wine
about 600ml/1 pint/2½ cups game or
   chicken stock (broth) (see page 49)
2 bay leaves
1 teaspoon chopped fresh rosemary
1 tablespoon chopped fresh sage
450g/1lb dry *pappardelle* or flat
   noodles, cooked
salt and freshly ground black pepper

1 Cut all the meat off the hare with a sharp knife. Cut the meat into small dice. (Alternatively you can joint the hare, brown the joints and simmer in the sauce, then remove the meat from the bones, mixing it into the cooking juices – I find my method easier!)

2 Heat the oil and butter in a sauté pan. Add the onion, carrot, celery and garlic. Stir well. Cook gently for 10 minutes until soft and beginning to brown.

3 Add the pancetta and hare, stir well and cook for a couple of minutes until the meat is browned. Season well. Stir in the flour, then the wine and half the stock (broth). Mix well, scraping any sediment lodged on the base of the pan. Add the herbs and bring to the boil. Turn down the heat, half cover and simmer gently for at least 2 hours, topping up with more stock (broth) as necessary, until the meat is tender and the sauce reduced.

4 Taste, season as necessary, remove the bay leaves and toss with buttered *pappardelle* or wide flat noodles. The sauce can be liquidized to make it finer.

Rabbit, hunter's style

Coniglio alla cacciatora

This recipe offers a simple way to give ordinary rabbit all the taste of the wild hills of Tuscany. The secret is in the reduction of the wine and the long slow cooking. In Tuscany, the farmed rabbits are huge and come with the heads and livers – these really make the sauce special. Cook the heads in the sauce then remove them, fry the livers quickly and purée with the sauce. My friend Alvaro likes nothing better than to eat the cooked rabbit heads, which he says are the best part. I've never had the courage myself!

SERVES 4–6

1 large rabbit, head removed but kept, livers
   kept, jointed into 8–12 pieces
4 large cloves garlic, finely chopped
1 tablespoon finely chopped rosemary
1 teaspoon salt
1 teaspoon cracked black pepper
1 bottle dry red wine
2 sprigs rosemary
3 tablespoons olive oil
2 tablespoons balsamic vinegar
2 tablespoons sun-dried tomato purée (paste)
a little stock (broth) or water

1 Wash and dry the rabbit joints. Mix the garlic, rosemary, salt and pepper together and rub well into the rabbit, especially the cut sides. Cover and allow to marinate for at least 2 hours.

2 Meanwhile pour the wine into a pan, add the rosemary sprigs and boil hard until reduced by half. Strain and cool.

3 Heat the oil in a large frying-pan and fry the rabbit joints, and the heads, until well browned all over. Remove to a casserole. Fry the livers in the pan and add to the rabbit.

4 De-glaze the pan with the balsamic vinegar, then add the wine, scraping up the sediment. Whisk in the tomato purée (paste), season bring to the boil and pour over the rabbit. Add a little water or stock (broth) if it isn't completely covered. Bring to the boil then simmer very gently for 45 minutes to 1 hour.

5 Lift the rabbit to a warm serving dish. Mash the livers into the sauce and reduce to a syrupy consistency, if necessary. Pour the sauce over the rabbit and serve with polenta or lemon-scented potatoes.

Medieval capon salad

Insalata de cappone

ALASTAIR LITTLE knows the secrets and importance of making a good stock (broth). Here he demonstrates how to perfectly poach a fowl (capons when you can get them) whilst making a rich stock (broth) for another dish. This salad has medieval origins.

SERVES 8

FOR THE CHICKEN BROTH:
(MAKES ABOUT 2 LITRES/3½ PINTS/8 CUPS):
1.5kg/3lb 5oz chicken wings
2 carrots, peeled and coarsely chopped
2 onions, peeled and coarsely chopped
1 head celery, chopped then washed
2 bay leaves, 1 sprig thyme, 1 sprig
    rosemary, a few parsley stalks, tied into
    a bouquet garni
6 chicken stock (bouillon) cubes
4 litres/7 pints/17½ cups water
½ bottle white wine

FOR THE SALAD:
free-range chicken, 2.5kg/5½lb in weight
250g/9oz/2 cups pine nuts, toasted lightly
a handful of parsley leaves, to serve

FOR THE DRESSING:
120ml/4fl oz/½ cup red wine vinegar
2 bay leaves
2 tablespoons caster (superfine) sugar
1 cinnamon stick
½ teaspoon ground black pepper
165g/5½oz/1 cup raisins
rind (zest) of 1 orange and 1 lemon, pared
    in strips
sea salt
200ml/7fl oz/scant 1 cup extra virgin
    olive oil, to serve

The title is a misnomer in that chicken is used in this recipe as it is difficult to find capons now, as were used in medieval days. The stock (broth) from this recipe is to be used for a good chicken soup another time, perhaps with fresh vegetables boiled in it or with noodles added. The best use for the poached chicken in this recipe, apart from in its own broth, is Insalata di cappone. *AL*

1 To make the stock (broth), firstly trim the chicken wings – open one out and you will see three sections: the wing tip, the middle joint and what appears to be a miniature drumstick. Separate at each joint. Scissors are good for this.
2 Put the chopped wings, vegetables and bouquet garni in a stockpot. Add the stock (bouillon) cubes and water and bring to the boil. Lower the heat when it boils and add the wine. Stir and skim, cook at the barest simmer for 3 hours and skim.
3 To cook the chicken for the salad, plunge the bird into the unsieved stock (broth) and turn the heat up to medium. As it nears the boil, turn to low again, skim and simmer gently for 1 hour, adding water to cover the chicken if needed. Cover with a drop lid. Skim again, take off the heat and allow the chicken to cool in its stock (broth). Remove the chicken with a spider (mesh spoon), wrap and refrigerate.
4 To finish off the stock (broth), sieve and discard all the solids, and return to the cleaned-out pan, then bring to a rapid boil. As it boils remove the scum. After the first skim, add 500ml/17fl oz/just over 2 cups cold water, bring back to the boil and skim. This removes fat for a clear soup. Continue to boil and skim until reduced by half. Allow to cool and refrigerate or freeze.
5 For the salad dressing, put the vinegar in a pan and bring to the boil, then add the bay leaves, sugar, cinnamon, pepper, raisins and rind (zest). Stir until the sugar is dissolved and leave over a very low heat to infuse.
6 Shred the chicken meat into a large bowl discarding all skin, fat and bone. Add the pine nuts to the chicken. Return the vinegar mix to the boil, remove the bay leaves and cinnamon. Pour this mix over the chicken, season with sea salt, and toss well. Refrigerated for up to 3 days to improve the flavours. To serve, remove from the refrigerator 1 hour before serving. Add olive oil and the parsley leaves and toss.

7

Meat
Dishes

Milanese ossobuco

Ossobuco alla Milanese

ANNA DEL CONTE is one of the world's most respected food writers, particularly with regard to northern Italian food and cooking. This is her expert recipe for the classic and authentic *ossobuco alla Milanese*. *Ossobuco* comes from the hind leg of a calf and ideally should be no more than 4cm/1 ½ in thick. This is truly a delicious recipe!

SERVES 4

4 *ossobuchi*, about 250g/9oz each
2 tablespoons olive oil
flour, for dusting
40g/1½ oz/3 tablespoons butter
1 small onion, finely chopped
½ stick celery, finely chopped
150ml/¼ pint/⅔ cup dry white wine
300ml/½ pint/1¼ cups meat stock (broth)
    (see page 49)
salt and freshly ground black pepper

FOR THE *GREMOLADA*:

1 teaspoon grated rind (zest) from an
    unwaxed lemon
½ clove garlic, very finely chopped
2 tablespoons chopped fresh flat-leaf parsley

The traditional ossobuco alla Milanese *does not contain tomatoes. In fact, few Milanese dishes contain tomatoes or tomato sauce. As with Veneto or Piedmontese cooking, tomato hardly ever became part of the traditional repertoire. The reason is obvious – no tomatoes grow in these most northerly regions of Italy. Also, think of the traditional accompaniment to* ossobuco alla Milanese. *It is* risotto alla Milanese, *which is Risotto with saffron (see page 75). Saffron and tomato sauce do not go together, nor does tomato sauce go with the delicious* gremolada *added at the end of the cooking, the taste of which must come through against the winey flavour of the meat, and nothing else. ADC*

1 Tie the *ossobuchi* around and across with string as you would a parcel. Choose a heavy sauté pan, with a tight-fitting lid, large enough to hold the *ossobuchi* in a single layer. Heat the oil, and meanwhile lightly coat the *ossobuchi* with some flour in which you have mixed a teaspoon of salt. Brown the *ossobuchi* on both sides and then remove to a side dish.

2 Add 30g/1oz /2 tablespoons of the butter to the sauté pan together with the onion and the celery. Sprinkle with a little salt, which will help the onion to release its liquid so that it gets soft without browning. When the vegetables are soft – after about 10 minutes – return the meat to the pan along with the juice that will have accumulated. Heat the wine and pour over the meat. Turn the heat up and boil to reduce by half, while scraping the bottom of the pan with a metal spoon.

3 Heat the stock (broth) in the pan you used to heat the wine and pour about half over the *ossobuchi*. Turn the heat down to very low and cover the pan.

4 Cook for 1½–2 hours, until the meat has begun to come away from the bone. Carefully turn the *ossobuchi* over every 20 minutes or so, taking care not to damage the marrow in the bone. If necessary, add more stock (broth) during the cooking, but very gradually – not more than 3 or 4 tablespoons at a time. If, by the time the meat is cooked, the sauce is too thin, remove the meat from the pan and reduce the liquid by boiling briskly.

5 Transfer the *ossobuchi* to a heated dish and remove the string. Keep warm in a cool oven. Cut the remaining butter into 3 or 4 pieces and add gradually to the sauce. As soon as the butter has melted, remove from the heat, as the sauce should not boil. This addition of the butter will give the sauce a glossy shine and a very delicate taste.

6 Mix the ingredients for the *gremolada* together, stir into the sauce and leave for a minute or two. After that, just spoon the sauce over the *ossobuchi* and serve immediately.

TIP: Buy *ossobuchi* that are the same size so they cook for the same amount of time.

Slow-cooked beef stew from Friuli-Venezia Giulia

Gulasch

CLAUDIO PECORARI presents his version of *gulasch* (or *gulyas*), a classic meat dish that originates in Hungary. This recipe, and other Middle Euopean influences, found their way into the Italian cuisine when Trieste, which used to be the main port for the Austro-Hungarian Empire, became part of Italy in 1954.

SERVES 4

100g/4oz minced *lardo* (lard or pork backfat), or prosciutto fat
4 tablespoons strong/hot paprika
2 tablespoons plain (all-purpose) flour
1kg/2 ¼ lbs lean silverside of beef or topside of beef, cubed
1kg/2 ¼ lbs onions, sliced
2 teaspoons chopped fresh rosemary
1 teaspoon chopped fresh thyme
1 tablespoon chopped fresh marjoram
1 bay leaf
100g/4oz/⅓ cup tomato purée (paste)

This recipe developed at the beginning of my career in the kitchen, when I was working under Lucio, a very traditional chef, at the Trattoria all'Adriatico in Trieste. It was a very famous restaurant at that time, with an extremely rich traditional clientele (the remnants of a faded empire)! This is a northern Italian dish with Eastern European influences. CP

1 Slowly melt the *lardo* in a casserole over a low heat.
2 Mix the flour and paprika together in a bowl. Add the cubed meat and toss until well-coated and separate.
3 Add the meat to the casserole, raise the heat and stir well, sealing and browning the meat. (You can do this in batches.)
4 Add the onions and keep stirring. Don't worry if it looks like is burning the bottom of the pan – soon the onion will release its juices and pick the bits up from the bottom. Add the chopped herbs and keep stirring so it doesn't stick. This will take about 20 minutes.

5 Mix the tomato purée (paste) with about 1 litre/1¾ pints/4 cups of water and pour it over the meat. Stir and cover, and turn the heat to the minimum or to barely simmering and cook for a further 45 to 60 minutes until the meat is *al dente* or only just separating.
6 With a 'spider' or slotted spoon, take the meat out of the sauce and put it in a warm serving plate. Pass the sauce through a mouli (food mill) or strainer and serve ladled over the meat, ideally with *Gnocchi di patate* (see page 82), the delicious Potato *gnocchi* recipe, also provided by myself.

Calves' liver and onions, Venetian-style

Fegato alla Veneziana

ALASTAIR LITTLE guides us through another classic dish. Cooking really good calves' liver is tricky, and he shows us, amongst other things, how the onions should be meltingly soft and sweet.

SERVES 4

500g/1lb 2oz calves' liver, thinly sliced
and skinned
2 tablespoons butter
a little extra virgin olive oil
500g/1lb 2oz onions, peeled and finely sliced
4 sage leaves
a handful chopped parsley
salt and freshly ground black pepper
2 lemons, halved, to serve

This classic Italian liver dish is best known outside Italy. The marriage of liver and onions is one made in heaven, it can't be bettered, and like all the best liaisons does not brook tampering or interference. The secret to cooking the liver is to keep the cooking brief, and not to cook it too fiercely because when the surface scorches, it has an unpleasant taste and rather rank charred odour. Calves' liver is pale, tender and mild in flavour. It frequently converts liver-haters to its cause, but is rather expensive. You may have to search for it or bully your butcher to order it for you. Also, ask your butcher to trim and slice it thinly; you will need approximately 125–175g/4–6oz per person. He (or she) can leave the outer skin on each slice to help keep the slices firm when cutting but ask him to remove the skin after he's cut the slices – it's an unpleasant task. AL

1 You will need a large frying pan. Cut the liver into ribbons 5–6cm/2½in long and 5mm/¼in across. Season well.
2 Take a large frying pan and melt half the butter with a little oil over a medium heat. Add the onions and sage, stir and turn down the heat, then allow the onion to soften and go translucent for about 15 minutes or so with the sage leaves.

3 Turn the heat up to medium and add the liver. Cook, occasionally turning the liver, for 4–5 minutes until the liver has stiffened slightly and coloured. Throw in the remaining butter and add the parsley. Check the seasoning and serve with lemon halves. This recipe is also very delicious with creamy mashed potatoes or some soft polenta.

Beef braised in Barolo

Brasato al Barolo

Barolo is a truly great full-bodied red wine from Piedmont, which is ready to drink when it is at least 3–4 years old. It turns a deep red brown colour with age and is made from the Nebbiolo grape. Normally a whole piece of beef is marinated in hearty Barolo wine, then slowly braised and served sliced with the puréed sauce. In my version, the wine is reduced before cooking to concentrate the flavour and the meat is cut into large chunks. The sauce is dark and luxurious after the long slow cooking. This is a very good dish for a dinner party.

SERVES 6–8

2 bottles good quality Barolo or other good
   red wine
1.5kg/3lb 5oz stewing beef such as shin,
   chuck, or skirt
2 onions, roughly chopped
2 carrots, chopped
1 stick celery, chopped
2 bay leaves
2 large sprigs fresh thyme
6 peppercorns
2 allspice berries
3 tablespoons olive oil
2 tablespoons tomato (or sun-dried)
   purée (paste)
1 litre/1¾ pints/4 cups beef stock (broth)
   (see page 49)
salt and freshly ground black pepper
chopped parsley, to serve

1 Pour the wine into a large saucepan or sauté pan and bring to the boil. Boil hard until reduced by half to 750ml/1¼ pints/ 3 cups. Cool completely.

2 Trim the meat of any fat or gristle and cut into 6.5cm/2½in pieces. Place in a large polythene bag with the onion, carrot, celery, bay leaves, thyme, peppercorns and crushed allspice berries. Pour in the cooled wine. Shake the bag to mix, seal and marinate in the refrigerator overnight.

3 Open the bag and pour the contents into a colander or sieve placed over a bowl. Remove the meat and pat dry with kitchen paper. Reserve the wine.

4 Heat the oil in a large flameproof casserole and brown the meat well in batches. Return the meat into the casserole and stir in the vegetables, herbs and spices.

5 Pour over the reserved marinade wine and stir in the tomato purée (paste). Add enough stock (broth) to cover the meat and vegetables. Bring to the boil, turn down the heat, cover and simmer gently for 2–3 hours or until the meat is very tender. Or, cook in the oven at 170°C/ 325°F/Gas 3 for 2–3 hours. Top the liquid up with extra stock (broth) if needed.

6 Lift the meat out of the casserole with a slotted spoon and place in a bowl. Remove the bay leaves from the sauce. Pour the sauce into a liquidizer or food processor and blend until smooth. The sauce will look pale, but will darken when reheated. Taste and season. The sauce should be quite thick, if not, boil to reduce it.

7 Stir the meat into the sauce and reheat until piping hot. Serve sprinkled with some parsley.

Little veal, prosciutto and sage escalopes

Saltimbocca

This is a classic way of cooking veal escalopes to 'jump into the mouth'. You'll find people standing around the stove waiting for the next one to jump out of the pan before it lands on the plate, which is what happens when you cook these. They are addictive!

SERVES 4

8 x 125g/4½oz veal escalopes (turkey
    escalopes work just as well)
8 slices *prosciutto* or Parma ham
8 fresh sage leaves
seasoned flour, for dusting
125g/4½oz/8 tablespoons butter
200ml/7fl oz/scant 1 cup dry Marsala
    or sherry
salt and freshly ground black pepper
fresh sage leaves, to garnish

1 Trim the escalopes of any gristle around the edge. Place between sheets of cling film (plastic wrap) and bat out thinly without tearing.

2 Season each escalope with a little salt. Lay a slice of ham on each escalope and a sage leaf on top. Secure through the middle like taking a large stitch with a cocktail stick. These are not rolled up. Dust the escalopes with some seasoned flour on both sides.

3 Heat half the butter in a frying pan and fry the escalopes four at a time, for 2 minutes a side until golden brown and tender. Remove and keep warm.

4 Add the Marsala to the pan, stir scraping any sediment from the base of the pan and bring to the boil. Add the remaining butter and boil rapidly for 1 minute. Spoon the sauce over the escalopes and serve immediately with the sage leaves.

Bollito misto

Bollito misto

ALASTAIR LITTLE presents his masterful recipe for one of the most classic and spectacular of Italian dishes. The ingredients are simple, but the preparation lengthy – this is the secret of its perfection. Be warned, it takes more than a day!

SERVES 10

(The quantities here provide a feast for 10, but will comfortably feed 20. If serving large numbers, increase the vegetables so everyone gets an onion, a carrot and a leek. This dish really has to be cooked in large quantities and does not work in scaled-down versions).

13 onions
10 carrots
13 sticks celery
4.5kg/10lbs assorted veal or beef bones, sawn into pieces
2 tablespoons sunflower oil
1 calf's foot (ask your butcher to singe the hairs off)
1 bottle red wine (750ml/26fl oz/3$\frac{1}{4}$ cups)
4 bay leaves
1 shin of beef in a round, weighing about 900g/2lbs and tied in a neat joint
2 shins of veal, each weighing 675g/1$\frac{1}{2}$lbs), tied into neat joints
2 veal knuckles, sawn off the end of the shins
1 pickled ox tongue
1 2.7–3.5kg /6–8lb capon-type chicken
10 medium-sized leeks
1 *zampone* or *cotechino* sausage
10 medium-sized boiling potatoes (optional)

TO SERVE:

2 x quantity *salsa verde* (see page 42)
1 x quantity *mostarda di venezia* (see page 188)

Behind its prosaic title, which really means 'boiled meats', lies one of the great dishes of the global kitchen, and the Italian variation of the 'pot au feu'. Essentially a dish from Piedmont, it is today a house speciality that people in Italy still go a long way to find. Restaurants which offer it have special steel serving chariots with individual compartments for the beef, veal, tongue, chicken and zampone or cotechino *sausage which are all carved at the table. As well as the broth that is ladled over, the carved meats are accompanied by boiled root vegetables and a sharp-tasting* salsa verde, *which cuts the richness of the different flesh elements. Sometimes a* salsa rossa *or* red pepper sauce *is served too, as well as* mostarda di cremona – *sweet but hot mustard fruits, now widely available (see the* mostarda di venezi *recipe). This dish is a version of the* bollito misto *we serve in my restaurant, where it takes three days to prepare, and is a labour of love, strictly for people who like to eat lots of meat. Plain boiled potatoes go well with it.*

However, lengthy preparation does not mean it is difficult to achieve. Your hard work will be amply rewarded with a spectacular lunch or dinner, and excellent cold cuts for days afterwards. You will also have several litres of stock (broth) left over, which you can reduce and freeze. The leftover meat can also be served as a soup made from the stock (broth) and vegetables, with a little leaf spinach blanched and added at the end for colour and freshness. AL

1 Day 1. Preheat the oven to 190°C/375°F/Gas 5. Peel 3 onions, 3 carrots and 3 sticks celery and chop them all into 1cm/$\frac{1}{2}$in pieces. Brush the veal or beef bones with oil and put them in a roasting tin (pan) with the diced vegetables. Roast the bones for 1$\frac{1}{2}$ hours, turning from time to time and checking that they are not burning. Put the calf's foot in a pan and cover with cold water. Bring to the boil, skim and drain, then refresh in cold water. Put the roasted bones and vegetables into a large pot, cover with cold water and put over a high heat. Deglaze the roasting tin (pan) with the red wine, scraping up all the caramelized bits from the bottom and add to the stock pot.

2 When the stock (broth) boils, skim and turn down the heat Add the bay leaves and season lightly. Simmer for 6 hours,

skimming at regular intervals and adding more water as necessary to compensate for evaporation. The bones should always be covered with stock (broth). At the end of this time, add the calf's foot tied with a long piece of string left hanging out of the pot so that it can be retrieved easily.

3 After another 1 hour, retrieve the calf's foot and reserve in the refrigerator. Using a large ladle, strain the stock (broth) through a sieve into a large container. Discard the last few ladlefuls of stock (broth) with the bones and vegetables. Wash out the stock pot and strain the stock (broth) into it through a fine sieve. Put on a high heat and bring to the boil. Watch carefully. As it comes to the boil the fat will collect to one side of the pot where it and the impurities will be briefly trapped, building up into a scum.

Remove it immediately and pour in 575ml/1 pint/2½ cups of cold water. Repeat the process, then return the finished stock (broth) to a boil and turn off the heat. Leave to cool on the hob without any other burners on and away from a hot oven. Ventilate the area if possible. You really want a cool environment to avoid any risk of bacterial contamination.

4 Day 2. Tie retrieving strings to the beef and veal joints. Put the ox tongue to soak in plenty of cold water overnight. Return the stock to the boil, lower the heat immediately to a bare simmer and add the shin of beef and the calf's foot. Simmer for 1 hour, then add the veal shins and knuckles and continue to simmer for another 30 minutes. Add the chicken and simmer all the meats together for another 1½ hours. (That is, a total cooking time of 3 hours.) Transfer all the pieces of meat to a suitable container, cool, then refrigerate. Pick over the calf's foot at this stage, discarding all the bones. You will be left with several large pieces of gelatinous flesh. Refrigerate these with the rest of the meat. Return the stock to a boil and skim as before. Cool as before.

5 Day 3. Wash and trim the leeks. Peel the remaining carrots, celery and onions, reserving the trimmings. Drain the ox tongue, put it a pan and cover with cold water. Bring to the boil. Taste: if it is salty, discard the water then replace with fresh water and repeat. Add the vegetable trimmings, return to the boil and then simmer over a medium heat for 2 hours, or until a carving fork inserted into the tongue is easy to withdraw: if the tongue slides off easily then it is done: if the meat grips the fork it needs more cooking. Drain the tongue and leave to cool for 10 minutes. Then peel off the rough outer skin. This is easy to do while it is still fairly hot but very difficult if you allow it to cool too much.

6 Divide the leeks into 2 bundles and tie them with string. Bring the stock to a simmer and poach all the vegetables until done, removing each and refreshing in cold water. Cooking the vegetables in this way will help cut the richness of the stock (broth), which by now will have become intensely meaty.

7 Poach the sausage still in its foil wrapper in simmering water according to the manufacturer's instructions. If you plan to serve boiled potatoes, then peel and cook in the water around the sausage. Turn the oven on to a low heat and put a large roasting dish to warm in it. Also warm a largest serving dish.

8 At last the final stage is upon you and your guests (who should have been advised to starve for a day) will be assembled. Cut the strings off the leeks and put all the vegetables into a pan and moisten with stock. Unwrap the sausage from its foil wrapper. Do this over a dish as fat will gush out. Now cut one 5mm/ ¼ in slice of each meat for each person and assemble in batches so you have the right number of servings. (Don't use the ends from the meats: these can be kept for soup to have another day.) If necessary, adjust the seasoning of the stock (which should not be boiling, but very hot). Using a blanching basket, dip each batch of meat into the stock. Transfer to the hot roasting tray, moistening the meat with ladlefuls of stock (broth) until all the servings are ready. The whole process will only take 5 minutes. Cover with foil and put in the low oven for another 5 minutes.

9 To serve, drain the vegetables and mound them in the centre of the warmed serving dish. Then arrange the sliced meats from the roasting dish around them. Ladle over a little more stock (broth). Serve immediately with the *salsa* and *mostarda*.

TIPS: Serve lots of good full-bodied red wine, like Barolo. Serve flaky sea salt and different mustards as well as the *salsa verde* and *mostarda*. Don't make *bollito misto* in the summer, when a high ambient temperature threatens the cooling stock (broth). Don't invite vegetarians to the feast! Don't serve a starter. Don't serve a dessert – just fruit and, perhaps, a piece of Reggiano Parmesan cheese.

Roast pork loin with rosemary and garlic

Arista di maiale con finocchio

When this dish is cooking the aroma takes me back to the early morning markets in Tuscany, where the porchetta *stalls display whole roast pigs, heavily scented with garlic and rosemary, that have been cooked all night in a wood-fired oven. The meat is sliced and stuffed into thick buns with a bit of crackling! It is how to cook it at home. It is my version of* Arista alla fiorentina, *which I serve to my guests at Fattoria Montellucci in Tuscany, often cooking it in the cooling bread oven after baking pizzas.*

SERVES 6

1.75kg/3¾ lb loin of pork
6 large cloves garlic
4 tablespoons chopped fresh rosemary
2 teaspoons fennel seeds
300ml/½ pint/1¼ cups dry white wine
4 sprigs fresh rosemary
1 tablespoon olive oil
salt and freshly ground black pepper

1 Preheat the oven to 220°C/450°F/Gas 8. Ask the butcher to bone the loin, but to give you the bones. Also ask him to remove the skin and score it, which will create the crackling.

2 Turn the loin fat side down. Make deep slits all over the meat especially in the thick part.

3 Make a paste of the garlic, rosemary, fennel seeds, and at least a teaspoon each of salt and pepper (more will give a truly authentic Tuscan flavour) in a food processor. Push this paste into all the slits in the meat and spread the remainder over the surface of the meat. Roll up and tie with fine string.

4 Weigh the meat and calculate the cooking time allowing 25 minutes to every 500g/1lb. Brown all over in a frying pan then set in a roasting tin (pan) and pour the wine over the pork. Tuck in the extra rosemary sprigs.

5 Place the bones in another roasting pan convex side up. Rub the pork skin with a little oil and salt. Drape over the pork bones. Place the pan of crackling on the top shelf of the oven, and the pork on the bottom to middle shelf. Roast for about 20 minutes in the preheated oven, then turn down the heat to 200°C/400°F/Gas 6, and roast for the remaining calculated time, basting the pork every 20 minutes.

6 When cooked, serve the pork thickly sliced with shards of crunchy crackling and no gravy other than the juices from the roasting tin (pan).

Italian meatballs cooked in tomato sauce

Polpetti al sugo

MARY CONTINI has roots in southern Italy, where *sugo di ragù* (slow cooked tomato sauce) is often used to dress pasta and is very much part of family life. This is a recipe for classic meatballs cooked with tomato sauce – long slow cooking is the secret. It is really delicious!

SERVES 4–6

FOR THE TOMATO SAUCE:

2 tablespoons extra virgin olive oil
1 small onion, very finely chopped
1 clove garlic, peeled and chopped
small piece dried chilli
2 x 400g/14oz cans good quality
   Italian tomatoes
cooked spaghetti, to serve

FOR THE MEATBALLS:

400g/14oz best beef steak minced (ground)
   or 200g/7oz beef steak and 200g/7oz pork
   minced (ground) together
2–3 tablespoons breadcrumbs, freshly grated
   from dry bread
2 tablespoons freshly grated Parmesan
1 tablespoon finely chopped flat-leaf parsley
1 small onion, finely grated
1 tablespoon raisins (optional)
1 large free-range egg
3 tablespoons extra virgin olive oil
sea salt and freshly ground black pepper
vegetables or salad, to serve

These are little hand-rolled balls of minced (ground) beef, flavoured with herbs and seasonings. Nonna, (my grandmother) always asked the butcher to mince (grind) fillet steak especially for her polpetti. *This is a little extravagant, I admit, but do ask the butcher to mince (grind) lean stewing or rump steak for you. Ready-made mince will undoubtedly be too fatty. MC*

1 Make the tomato sauce. Warm the olive oil in a heavy-bottomed saucepan. Add the chopped onion, garlic and dried chilli, stir it around and sauté it very slowly unil the onion is soft and transparent. (This is called a *soffrito* and is the basis of many recipes in Italian cooking).

2 Smooth and de-seed the tomatoes by passing them through a mouli-legumes (food mill) or a fine sieve and stir into the *soffrito*. Bring to a very slow simmer while you make the meatballs.

3 Mix the beef, breadcrumbs, Parmesan and parsley together in a bowl. Add the finely grated onion. Add the raisins and plenty of seasoning and mix everything together. Season well – the mixture needs quite a bit of salt. Break the egg into the mixture and mix it in to bind the mixture.

4 Use clean hands to roll the mix into small balls, any size you like. Heat half the oil in a frying pan and brown the meatballs (in batches, adding more oil if needed.

5 Add the meatballs to the tomato sauce. Half cover and cook very slowly for about 1 hour, until the sauce is well-reduced. Adjust the seasoning at the end. Serve the *sugo* sauce tossed with spaghetti or *ziti* (long, fat maccheroni) and then serve the meatballs separately as a meat course with vegetables or salad.

Leg of lamb with lemon, oil and garlic

Coscia di agnello con limone, olio e aglio

FRANCESCA ROMINA offers a traditional family recipe here for cooking a large leg of lamb infused with the flavours of Sicily. Francesca suggests using a spring lamb – wait until after Easter for a really flavoursome lamb, when it has been grass-fed and is between 5 months and 1 year old. The older the lamb, the more fat there will be on the leg! Milk-fed lamb is rare and expensive; the legs are very small and it is not suitable for this long slow roasting method.

SERVES 4–6

2.75kg/6lb leg of spring lamb, trimmed of fat
10 large cloves garlic, quartered
4 tablespoons extra virgin olive oil
4 x 7.5cm/3in square lamb fat
   pieces, reserved

FOR THE LEMON, OIL AND GARLIC DRESSING:
juice of 5 lemons
120ml/4fl oz/½ cup extra virgin olive oil
10 cloves garlic, roughly chopped
2 teaspoons dried oregano, sticks removed,
   crushed until powdery
4 large potatoes, peeled and cut into
   2.5cm/1in thick slices
salt and freshly ground black pepper

Many Sicilian families traditionally eat lamb on Easter Sunday and other very special occasions. This recipe has been used in Sicily for centuries and is still made in Italian communities all over America. I suggest using a domestic spring lamb, which can weigh up to 7 pounds – avoid using New Zealand lamb, which has a gamey taste. Order the meat in advance from your local butcher. Vegetables such as corn on the cob, string beans, and broccoli make good side dishes. FR

1 Preheat an oven to 475°F/240°C/Gas 9. Cut 20 slits, each 2.5cm/1in long and 2.5cm/1in deep in the top of the leg of lamb. Cut 20 more slits on the bottom of the leg. Insert the garlic slivers into the slits, coat the bottom of a large roasting tin (pan) with the olive oil, then transfer the lamb and reserved fat into the roasting tin (pan).

2 In a small bowl, combine the lemon juice, olive oil, garlic, oregano and salt. Mix well. It can be made up to 3 days ahead of time and left refrigerated until needed. If the lemons are too acidic, add 1–2 tablespoons water.

3 Roast, uncovered, for 15 minutes at 240°C/475°F/Gas 9. Baste with the dressing, then reduce the heat to 180°C/350°F/Gas 4. Roast for 2 hours longer for rare lamb, or until an instant-read thermometer inserted into the centre registers 150°F; for 2½ hours longer for medium, or 160°F; or for 3 hours for well done, or 170°F.

4 During the last 1¼ hours of roasting, add the potatoes to the tin (pan). Baste the lamb and potatoes with the dressing and pan drippings every 20 minutes.

5 Transfer the lamb and potatoes to a large platter and allow the lamb to stand for 10 minutes before carving. Skim the excess fat off the pan juices and pour the juices into a gravy boat. Carve the lamb into slices and pass the gravy.

VARIATION: Prepare as directed, but omit the oregano in the dressing. Substitute 2 fresh Italian rosemary branches, each 30cm/12in long, for the oregano. Place 1 branch on each side of the lamb in the roasting tin (pan). Proceed as directed.

Devilled fillet steaks

Bistecca alla diavola con rucola

Italians love meat cooked very rare – especially in Tuscany. A great place to experience Tuscan steaks cooked over wood embers is Ristorante dei Laghi, near to the Fattoria Montellucci where we hold cookery classes. It is a carnivore's paradise – family run, warm and welcoming, and full of stuffed hunter's trophies. They cook the best bistecca alla fiorentina. *Unlike the simple cooking at dei Laghi, this recipe includes a very rich, piquant sauce, perfect with mature beef, although I've used their idea of serving sliced steak on a bed of rocket (arugula).*

SERVES 4

2 tablespoons olive oil

4 fillet steaks, about 175g/6oz each

2 tablespoons balsamic vinegar

6 tablespoons dry red wine

4 tablespoons really strong fresh beef stock (broth)

2 cloves garlic, chopped

1 teaspoon crushed fennel seeds

1 tablespoon sun-dried tomato purée (paste)

½ teaspoon crushed dried chilli pepper (or to taste)

200g/7oz wild rocket (arugula)

salt and freshly ground black pepper

chopped fresh parsley, to garnish

1 Heat the oil in a non-stick frying pan. When smoking hot, add the steaks and cook for 2 minutes, turn over and cook for 2 minutes more for medium/rare steaks.

2 Take the steaks out of the pan, season and keep warm. Pour the vinegar, red wine and stock (broth) into the pan and boil for 30 seconds, scraping any sediment from the base of the pan.

3 Add the garlic and fennel seeds. Whisk in the tomato purée (paste) and chilli. Bring to the boil and reduce until syrupy.

4 Transfer the steaks to a cutting board and thickly slice them. Quickly place a portion of rocket (arugula) on each of 4 warm plates and arrange the sliced meat on top. Pour any juices from the steaks into the sauce, bring to the boil, taste and season. Pour over the meat and serve immediately, garnished with some chopped parsley.

Pot roast, Florentine-style

Stracotto alla Fiorentina

PINO LUONGO presents this traditional Tuscan dish, which shows how a less expensive cut of meat can be made very tender by long slow cooking in a bath of aromatics and dried mushrooms.

SERVES 8

1.8 kg/4lbs silverside (eye round) beef
50ml/2fl oz/ ¼ cup olive oil
1 bulb fresh fennel, diced
2 white onions, diced
2 sticks celery, diced
2 carrots, diced
2 bay leaves
4 sprigs fresh thyme
4 leaves fresh sage
50g/2oz dried porcini mushrooms
1 bulb garlic, cut in half
1 bottle dry red wine
1 litre/1¾ pints/4½ cups of reduced
    veal or other meat stock (broth)
400g/14oz can chopped tomatoes
250g/9oz button or pickling (pearl)
    onions, peeled
salt and freshly ground black pepper

Stracotto *means 'overstewed'. When you see the prefix 'stra' in Italian, it means 'too much,' but here it doesn't have a negative meaning. The meat is so tender it should be almost falling apart. The recipe, which originated in Florence, is very, very good! PL*

1 Ask your butcher to trim all the excess fat from the meat, leaving just enough for braising. Preheat the oven to 200°C/400°F/Gas 6. Season the beef with salt and freshly ground black pepper.

2 Use a snug oval pan if you can, otherwise you will have to use a lot of liquid. Dampen the bottom of the pan with the olive oil and turn the heat to high. Sear the meat and brown well on all sides to keep the juices inside. There will be some smoke.

3 Remove the meat from the pan and set aside on a dish. Do not clean the pan when you remove the meat. What remains on the pan is the heart of this dish. It is important to use the pan juices in creating the correct taste. At this point, add the vegetables, herbs and the dried mushrooms. Sauté the vegetables for about 15 minutes stirring constantly: you want a nice caramelization to ensure the depth of flavour in the dish.

4 Once the vegetables are caramelized, add the bottle of wine. This will incorporate all the juices into the sauce. The wine must reduce by three-quarters; then add the veal or meat stock (broth). Add the canned tomatoes and the meat and bring to a boil. Remove from the heat, cover and place in the oven.

5 After 2 hours of braising the *stracotto* should be ready. You can check this by putting a fork in it; if the fork comes out without lifting the meat it is done. Remove the meat and strain the sauce (you may like to purée the sauce with the vegetables to thicken it). If the sauce becomes too thick, add water until it is to your liking. Then add the onions and simmer for about 10–20 minutes until tender.

6 Once the meat is sliced, place it on a plate cover it with some sauce and a few onions. Add some crusty Tuscan bread and you're in for a fantastic Italian feast!

8

Vegetables
and Salads

Italian tomato and egg torta

Crostata di pomodorini

VALENTINA HARRIS, renowned Italian cookery teacher, shows us this simple dish which demonstrates the Italian fondness of eggs and vegetables cooked together in an interesting way. The result is a delicious colourful type of omelette or *torta*, baked in the oven. Try this – it would make a great brunch dish.

SERVES 4

400g/14oz cherry tomatoes
2 tablespoons extra virgin olive oil
4 eggs
2 tablespoons plain (all-purpose) flour
200ml/7fl oz/scant 1 cup single (light) cream
   or crème fraîche
40g/1½oz/½ cup freshly grated Parmesan
40g/1½oz/½ cup freshly grated
   pecorino (romano)
a handful torn fresh basil
salt and freshly ground black pepper

This recipe makes the best use of the freshest baby tomatoes and farm eggs. Eggs in Italy are an amazing yellow colour due to the high content of maize in the diet – they produce golden pasta and really yellow omelettes. The contrast of the yellow of the eggs, the green of the basil and the red of the tomatoes make this dish a picture to look at. VH

1 Preheat the oven to 200°C/400°F/Gas 6.
2 Sprinkle the base of a lightly oiled non-stick 20cm/8in flan or pizza tin (pan) with a little of the grated cheese.
3 Wash and dry the tomatoes and arrange them over the base of the tin (pan) with a couple of tablespoons of oil.

4 Beat the eggs, cheeses and basil together and season. Pour over the tomatoes and bake for 20 to 25 minutes until firm and golden. Serve hot or cold, straight from the tin (pan), or turned out on to a platter.

Apulian bean purée

'Ncapriata

CLAUDIA RODEN'S recipe for a bean purée or dip is typical of bean dishes that have been made throughout southern Italy for centuries. They are sometimes made to be very runny and eaten as a soup. This is a taste as old as time!

SERVES 4

300g/11oz/2 cups dried broad (fava) beans
(buy them already skinned)
2 sticks celery, strings removed and
finely chopped
1 large potato, chopped
2 medium onions, finely chopped
120ml/4fl oz/½ cup or more extra virgin
olive oil
salt

Dried broad (fava) bean purée was always poor food – the kind peasants took to the fields. Even in Roman times it was given to slaves and gladiators. Now it is very popular again and chic in Apulia, Sicily and Calabria. In Calabria, where it is called macco di fave, *and in Sicily, where it is* maccu, *the bean purée is combined with cooked pasta such as* tagliolini *or* paternostri *or with rice, while in Sardinia it is combined with tomatoes and cardoons and called* favata. 'Ncapriata *partners the bland taste of the beans with bitter wild chicory or with spring onions and peppers. Although it is quite thick, it is served in Italy as a* minestra *or soup, but it is just as good as a dip with bread or* grissini. *CR*

1 Soak the beans in water overnight.
2 Drain and rinse the beans and put them in a saucepan with the celery, potato and onions. Cover with water and cook on a low heat for about two hours, stirring from time to time.
3 During the last stages of cooking add salt and a little oil, mixing well. Put the

mixture through a food mill or a food processor, then beat in more olive oil until you have a smooth, light consistency.

NOTE: This purée is usually served with boiled wild chicory – you could use curly endive, dressed in oil. Or serve with fried peppers, onions and tomatoes.

Beetroot and radicchio salad

Insalata di barbabietole e radicchio

VIANA LA PLACE is a master of salad combinations. This salad has northern origins, again demonstrating the love of a contrast in flavour and texture.

SERVES 4

4–5 small beetroots, about 3cm/1½in diameter, with tops attached
1 medium radicchio head
40g/1½oz fresh walnuts, coarsely chopped
3 tablespoons extra virgin olive oil
1 tablespoon red wine vinegar
1 tablespoon balsamic vinegar
salt and freshly ground black pepper

With its scarlet-on-scarlet colouring, this exquisite salad features contrasting textures of tender beetroots, crisp radicchio and rich walnuts. The beetroots are baked in the oven until tender – a method of cooking that concentrates their sweetness – then sliced paper thin. A spoonful of balsamic vinegar adds mellowness to the dressing and reinforces the sweetness of the beetroots. This elegant and festive salad is ideal for a Christmas dinner. Serve it separately from other foods, always a good policy with beetroot, since everything they touch turns a deep pink. Look for small beetroots with fresh leafy tops. The leaves are delicious cut into strips and sautéed in olive oil and garlic. VLP

1 Preheat the oven to 230°C/450°F/Gas 8. Trim all but about 1cm/½in from the tops of the beetroot, and if the leaves look fresh, reserve them and cook as above.
2 Wrap the beetroots in (aluminum) foil, tightly sealing the ends to form an envelope. Transfer the beetroots to a baking tray (sheet) and place in the preheated oven. Cook until tender but slightly resistant when pierced with a skewer. Unwrap the foil and, when cool, peel and slice the beetroots very thinly.
3 Cut the radicchio in half lengthways and wash under cold running water. Dry well. Cut out the core and cut the leaves into slivers.

4 Place the beetroots in the centre of a round serving platter. Surround with the slivered radicchio. Sprinkle the walnuts over the top of the salad. Drizzle with the olive oil and the two vinegars, and season with salt and pepper to taste. Either present the salad arranged on the serving plate and toss it in front of your guests, or toss the salad before bringing it to the table. Both presentations can be equally attractive.

Fennel, endive and orange salad with black olive dressing

Insalata di finocchio, arancia e scarola

Salads like these are typical of southern Italian cooking. The essence of this dish is the contrast of crunchy and soft textures, sweet and bitter flavours. Salads are served after the main course as a palate cleanser, and this one is very popular with my guests after a particularly 'fishy' meal. The thinly sliced fennel softens when marinated in this earthy citrus and olive dressing. The addition of curly endive makes this salad very refreshing.

SERVES 4

FOR THE DRESSING:
finely grated rind (zest) and juice of 1 orange
6 tablespoons extra virgin olive oil
2 tablespoons finely shredded fresh basil
2 tablespoons finely chopped, Greek-style
    black olives, stoned
2 sun-dried tomatoes in oil, finely chopped
salt and freshly ground black pepper

2 oranges
2 Florence fennel bulbs (with lots of
    green fronds)
125g/4½oz, curly endive, escarole or frisée

1 Mix all the dressing ingredients together in a large bowl. Season and leave to stand for a short while to let the ingredients develop their flavours.
2 Peel the oranges with a sharp knife, removing all the skin and pith. Cut out the segments. Set aside in a bowl. Trim the stalks and fronds from the fennel. Discard the stalks, but keep the green fronds.

3 Halve the fennel bulbs. Cut out the hard core, then finely slice using a very sharp thin-bladed knife. Immediately toss in the dressing with the orange segments to prevent discoloration. Leave to marinate in a cool place for 15 minutes.
4 Wash and dry the curly endive. Carefully mix with the fennel and transfer to a clean bowl. Serve immediately.

Courgettes (zucchini) and carrots '*a scapece*'

Zucchini e carote a scapece

You know you are eating southern Italian food when you taste this – I have eaten versions of it all over southern Italy. It is a particular favourite in Sicily where it is always flavoured with mint. It is a much loved combination of sweet and sour with the addition of sharp capers. 'A scapece' is a method of preserving using vinegar. The courgettes (zucchini) and carrots have to brown and caramelize before adding the reduced vinegar and mint. A very simple dish, but fundamental to the cuisine.

SERVES 4

4 tablespoons olive oil
3 medium courgettes (zucchini), thinly sliced
3 medium carrots, thinly sliced
2 tablespoons white wine vinegar
2 tablespoons shredded fresh mint
1 tablespoon salted capers, rinsed and
  roughly chopped
salt and freshly ground black pepper
extra mint sprigs, to garnish

1 Heat the oil in a frying pan and sauté the vegetables in batches until golden brown. Remove to a serving dish with a slotted spoon as they are ready, leaving any oil in the bottom of the pan. Season with salt and pepper.

2 Add the vinegar and mint to the pan and bring to the boil, then immediately pour this over the vegetables and toss carefully. Leave at room temperature for at least 30 minutes to develop the flavours. Scatter with capers and garnish with mint.

Roast potatoes with lemon and garlic

Patate arroste con aglio e limone

The potato is also a relative newcomer to Italy and was discovered in the New World. Until the nineteenth century it was used as an animal food, then a monk wrote a treatise on how to cook the tubers. One cannot imagine Italian cuisine without it! This method locks in all the nutrients. The potatoes are browned then steamed in their own moisture, and crisped again. They are scented with lemon and garlic in a particularly southern Italian way. The potatoes must be waxy or they will fall apart during cooking.

SERVES 4

500g/1lb 2oz medium-sized waxy potatoes
   such as Desirée
6 tablespoons olive oil
4 cloves unpeeled garlic
a few sprigs thyme or rosemary
finely grated rind (zest) of 1 lemon
coarse sea salt

1 Cut the potatoes into quarters lengthways and cover with cold water to soak for 10 minutes. Drain then pat dry.
2 Heat 4 tablespoons of the oil in a flameproof casserole and when really hot, add the potatoes and garlic. Reduce the heat and brown the potatoes on all sides. Stir in the herbs and lemon rind (zest), cover and cook in their own steam for 15 minutes.

3 Remove the lid and turn the heat up to evaporate any water and crisp the potatoes. Stir in the remaining olive oil.
4 Tip into a warm serving dish and scatter with plenty of salt and more herbs. The idea of the cooked whole garlic cloves is to soften the garlic so that the pieces slip out of their skin easily and are spread on to mouthfuls of potato as you eat them.

Peperonata with salted anchovies

Peperonata con acciughe salate

(Bell) peppers were only introduced to Italy by the Spanish after they had discovered them in the New World. Peperonata *is a gorgeous silky stew of sweet pepper and tomatoes, relying on the freshness and ripeness of the ingredients. If you've ever made this with vegetables ripened in the hot southern Italian sun – it is unforgettable, simply bursting with sunshine! The secret is the addition of salted anchovies to cut the richness of the sweet vegetables. Serve this with a selection of vegetable dishes, grilled fish or a* frittata *(omelette).*

SERVES 4

3 tablespoons olive oil
2 medium onions, sliced
3 cloves garlic, chopped
2 medium yellow and 2 medium red (bell)
   peppers, halved and seeded
1kg/2¼ lbs fresh ripe tomatoes, skinned, or
   2 x 400g/14oz cans Italian chopped tomatoes
6 salted anchovies, split, bone removed
   and rinsed
salt and freshly ground black pepper

1 Heat the olive oil in a saucepan, add the onions and garlic and cook over a gentle heat for at least 20 minutes until golden and caramelized.
2 Cut the (bell) peppers into thick strips. Add to the onions, cover and cook for 10 minutes to soften.

3 Core, seed and chop the tomatoes. Chop the anchovies. Stir them into the (bell) pepper mixture with the anchovies. Simmer uncovered for 30–45 minutes until soft, thick and reduced. Taste and season with salt and pepper. Serve warm or at room temperature.

Frittata of spaghetti with tomato and basil

Frittata di spaghetti al pomodoro e basilico

PINO LUONGO demonstrates here that leftover pasta can be reworked into a completely new, fresh-tasting dish with the right amount of care and attention. This is typical of the thriftiness of Italian cooks – nothing is ever thrown away! Use an ovenproof frying pan for this recipe.

SERVES 4

225g/8oz dried spaghetti, cooked
450ml/16fl oz/2 cups tomato sauce
3 ripe plum tomatoes, diced
40g/1½ oz/½ cup freshly
    grated Parmesan
10 basil leaves (5 for garnish, 5 chopped and
    added to the mixture)
3 large whole eggs
3 tablespoons extra virgin olive oil
100g/4oz buffalo mozzarella (*mozzarella
    di bufala*)
salt and freshly ground black pepper

A frittata is a versatile dish, very like an omelette, that can be served at any time of the day; it is also an excellent forum for leftovers, especially for pasta of any shape. It is popular all over Italy. In this recipe we are using spaghetti; however, seasonal vegetables, cheeses, or any other shape of pasta can be substituted. PL

1 Pre-heat oven to 200°C/400°F/Gas 6. In a large bowl mix the spaghetti, tomato sauce, diced tomato, Parmesan cheese and chopped basil.

2 Break the eggs into a separate bowl and whisk together with a pinch of salt and plenty of freshly ground black pepper. Stir the eggs into the spaghetti mixture.

3 Heat a 30cm/12 in ovenproof, non-stick frying or sauté pan; add the olive oil and wait until it smokes.

4 Slowly pour the mixture into the frying or sauté pan, so the oil doesn't splatter. Shake the pan to even out the ingredients and cook for 3 minutes at high heat. Place the pan in the oven for 10 minutes or until the eggs are set.

5 Test with a toothpick and if it comes out clean then the *frittata* is cooked. Turn out on to a large platter and cover with the diced mozzarella and basil leaves while still warm.

Sweet and sour aubergine (eggplant) and vegetable stew

Caponata

This is one of Sicily's national dishes, and everyone makes it their own way! However, it must contain aubergines (eggplants), celery, tomato, capers, nuts and vinegar. A delicious sweet and sour vegetable stew or salad, it is served as an antipasto or as a vegetable. The name derives from the caupone *or sailors' inns where the salad would be made with 'hard tack' or hard sailors' biscuits soaked in vinegar to soften them. Today the soaked biscuit has disappeared from the ingredients – a blessing? As always in Sicily, serve at room temperature. My colleague and friend Carla Tomasi makes the best* caponata *I have ever tasted. If you have access to abundant supplies of olive oil, then fry the aubergines (eggplants) in that.*

SERVES 6

4 medium aubergines (eggplants), cut into
    bite-sized cubes
olive oil (see method)
1 medium onion, chopped
2 sticks celery, sliced
8 really ripe red tomatoes, roughly chopped,
    or 400g/14oz can Italian chopped tomatoes
3 tablespoons raisins
2 tablespoons salted capers, rinsed well
15 green olives, stoned
about 3 tablespoons red wine vinegar
about 1 tablespoon sugar
salt and freshly ground black pepper
toasted chopped almonds, to garnish
chopped parsley, to garnish

1 Place the aubergines (eggplants) in a colander, sprinkle with salt and leave to disgorge for 30 minutes.

2 Heat a little olive oil in a saucepan and add the onion and celery. Cook for 5 minutes until soft but not brown, add the tomatoes and raisins, and cook for 15 minutes until pulpy. Add all the remaining ingredients to the sauce and cook for 15 minutes.

3 Rinse and pat the aubergines (eggplants) dry. Deep fry in olive oil in batches until deep golden brown. This may take some time. Drain well.

4 Stir the aubergines (eggplants) into the sauce. Taste and adjust the seasoning. Allow to stand for at least 30 minutes to allow the flavours to develop before serving. Serve warm or tepid in a bowl topped with the almonds and parsley.

Roasted baby artichokes with catmint (catnip) salmoriglio

Carciofi arrostiti con nepitella e salmoriglio

ANNA TASCA LANZA presents this wonderful recipe for preparing artichokes with a type of wild mint. This mint is used wherever it grows throughout Italy and Tuscans often use it with wild mushrooms.

In Sicily, catmint (catnip) is used in the kitchen only in certain areas – on the island of Salina, for instance, it grows everywhere and cooks make great use of it. Along with capers, it features in almost all of their recipes. The genus name for catmint (nepeta) comes from the Etruscan town of Nepe, today called Nepi in the province of Viterbo. It is known as catmint because the smell intoxicates cats! The following recipe is for the artichokes that I preserve in jars. Our artichokes are similar to baby artichokes. They are thorny at the top of the leaves, so you have to pay attention not to prick yourself. ATL

SERVES 4

FOR THE *SALMORIGLIO*
3 cloves garlic, crushed
juice of 4 lemons (at least 120ml/4floz/¹⁄₂ cup)
50g/2oz/¹⁄₂ cup fresh catmint (catnip) leaves
    or 25g/1oz/¹⁄₄ cup mint leaves mixed with
    25g/1oz/¹⁄₄ cup oregano leaves
120ml/4fl oz/¹⁄₂ cup olive oil
salt and ground chilli pepper

2 lemons
2kg/4¹⁄₂lbs baby artichokes, outer leaves
    removed (see page 36)

1 Mix together all the ingredients for the *salmoriglio* and set aside.
2 Squeeze the juice of the lemons into a bowl of cold water. Cut the artichoke hearts in half, removing the choke if any. Put the halves immediately in the lemon water so that they don't turn dark.
3 Grill on a roasting pan on the grill, turning on all sides, until withered and brownish. When the artichokes are done, mix them in the *salmoriglio* while hot and let rest for a few minutes before serving. They keep in the refrigerator for 1 week.
4 If you have a lot, preserve them in sterilized jars. Place them in the jars and cover with half vegetable oil, half olive oil. Close the jars and place in a large bain-marie (hot water bath) and simmer for 20 minutes. Remove with tongs and leave to cool. They will last for ages.

Quick fresh garden stew

Stu rapido con verdure

FRANCESCA ROMINA is a Sicilian-New Yorker, and teaches the cuisine of her ancestral country in her Little Italy Cook School. She is so enthusiastic about the food of her home country and the freshness of the ingredients, and this dish encapsulates the peasant way of making a simple, delicious meal from whatever is in season, augmented by fresh eggs to make the dish more substantial. Sicilians love squash as well as courgettes (zucchini), particularly a pale green curly version that is cooked as a vegetable and made into a jam.

SERVES 4

675g/1½lbs medium-small green squash or
  courgettes (zucchini)
120ml/4fl oz/½cup extra virgin olive oil
1 medium-small yellow onion, thinly sliced
1 large potato, peeled and cut into
  1cm/½in cubes
120ml/4fl oz/½ cup – 250ml/8fl oz/1cup
  tomato sauce or 1 really ripe large
  tomato, peeled, seeded, and chopped
½ teaspoon oregano, stalks removed,
  crushed until powdery
10 large fresh basil leaves, torn into
  small pieces
4 large eggs
grated *caciocavallo, canestrato, provolone,*
  or pecorino (romano) cheese
salt and freshly ground black pepper

Cooks in Ciminna make this stew often as a way of using up their fresh vegetables, serving it for lunch or an evening snack with sandwiches, a frittata or leftovers. Whenever I cook this stew, I always make it red by adding tomato sauce or chopped fresh tomato. I also always add eggs, which is a Sicilian peasant tradition, and a way of making more of a meal. Squash grows abundantly in Sicily and can be found in every small garden. Sicilians prefer cucuzza, *a common green squash that resembles a cucumber. Courgettes (zucchini), in contrast, are light mint green, about one foot long, and slightly curled and can be used here as an alternative. Many people are sentimental about cooking mint green courgettes (zucchini) because they remember their grandmothers cooking them for them when they were children. But today courgettes (zucchini) are too often tough and not very sweet. On the plus side, they will not fall apart as easily as* cucuzza, *so many Sicilians use them for making a stew. FR*

1 Peel the squash or courgettes (zucchini), leaving on thin strips of the skin to create a striped appearance. Quarter each one lengthways, then cut crosswise into 2.5cm/1in pieces.
2 In a medium-sized pan, heat the olive oil over a medium heat. Add the onion and potato and sauté, sprinkling with a dash of salt and stirring occasionally, until the onion is golden and the potatoes begin to brown, about 8 minutes. Add the squash or courgette (zucchini) pieces and continue cooking, stirring occasionally, until they become golden – another 8 minutes.
3 Add the tomato sauce or chopped tomato and enough water to cover (about 1 litre/1¾ pints/3 or 4 cups) along with the oregano, basil, 1 teaspoon salt and ½ teaspoon black pepper. Bring the stew to a boil, reduce the heat to low, prop a spoon under the lid to keep the pot half uncovered, and simmer until the stew begins to thicken, about 20 minutes.
4 If using the eggs, crack them one by one and gently drop them into the stew; do not stir. Taste the stew every 10 minutes and adjust all the seasonings as necessary. Re-cover and continue simmering for another 15 to 20 minutes. Once the eggs have set and the potatoes are fork-tender, the stew is done. During the last 10 minutes of cooking, add 4 tablespoons grated cheese. Serve with more grated cheese and Sicilian bread.

9

Breads
and Pizzas

Basic pizza dough [v]

Use this to make pizza or a less refined focaccia *– the rye flour gives a more robust flavour to the dough – but you can use all plain (all-purpose) flour instead if rye is hard to find.*

MAKES 2 X 25–30CM/10–12IN THIN CRUST PIZZAS

25g/1oz fresh yeast, 15g/½oz dried active
   baking yeast, or 2 x 7g sachets easy-
   blend yeast
a pinch of sugar
250ml/8 fl oz/1cup warm water
500g/1lb 2oz/3⅓ cups Italian '00' flour or
   plain white (all-purpose) flour plus extra,
   for dusting
2 tablespoons olive oil, plus extra for brushing
   and drizzling
1 teaspoon salt

1 In a medium bowl, cream the fresh yeast with the sugar and whisk in the warm water. Leave for 10 minutes until frothy. For other yeasts, use according to manufacturer's instructions.

2 Sift the flour into a large bowl and make a well in the centre. Pour in the yeast mixture, olive oil and salt. Mix together with a round-bladed knife, then your hands until the dough comes together.

3 Tip out on to a floured surface, wash and dry your hands and knead for 10 minutes until smooth and elastic. The dough should be quite soft, but if too soft to handle, add more flour.

4 Place in a clean oiled bowl, cover with a damp tea towel and leave to rise until doubled – about 1 hour.

Breadsticks

Grissini [v]

Grissini *originate from Turin in northern Italy where the hand-made variety is preferred. These bear no resemblance to the ones in packets and are much superior in taste and texture. They are fun to make and are great served with drinks!*

MAKES ABOUT 40

½ quantity basic pizza dough (see
   recipe above)
crystal sea salt, sesame seeds, poppy seeds,
   cracked pepper or other flavourings,
   for sprinkling
slices of *prosciutto*, to serve (optional)

1 Roll the dough out thinly on a well-floured surface to a rectangle. Cut into 5 mm/¼in strips following the long side of the rectangle. Lightly roll these strips and taper the ends.

2 Brush lightly with water and sprinkle with the flavouring of your choice. Lay on a baking tray (sheet) and bake in a preheated oven at 200°C/400°F/Gas 6 for 5–8 minutes until crisp and brown. Cool completely.

3 Twist strips of *prosciutto* around the sticks, to serve, if you like, or leave plain for a vegetarian option.

White onion and mozzarella pizza

Pizza in bianca con cipolle e ulive

Pizza in bianca is a pizza with no hint of tomato sauce. This is a succulent pizza from the south where the onions are cooked to a creamy softness in olive oil before being spread on the pizza base, flavoured with herbs and anchovies and dotted with black olives.

MAKES 2 X 30CM/12IN PIZZAS

1 quantity basic pizza dough (see page 150)
6 tablespoons olive oil
1kg /2¼lbs onions, finely sliced
1 tablespoon chopped fresh rosemary
2 teaspoons dried oregano
1 mozzarella, drained and thinly sliced
2 tablespoons freshly grated Parmesan
12 anchovy fillets in oil, drained
15 black olives, stoned
salt and freshly ground black pepper
rosemary sprigs, to garnish

1 First prepare one quantity of pizza dough (see recipe).
2 Heat the oil in a saucepan and add the onions. Cook over a gentle heat for about 20 minutes, stirring occasionally, until the onions are completely soft and golden. They must not brown. Stir in the herbs and season.
3 Knock back the pizza dough. Divide the dough in two and roll out (or stretch with your fingers) to two 25–30cm/10–12in about 5mm/¼in thick. Slide these on to two well-floured flat baking trays (sheets).

4 Cover the pizza base with a sliced mozzarella before topping with the onions. Sprinkle with the Parmesan. Scatter over the anchovy fillets and olives.
5 Bake for 15–20 minutes in a preheated oven 240°C/475°F/Gas 9 until golden and crisp. Scatter with rosemary sprigs and serve immediately.

Potato, sausage and ricotta double-crust pizza

Sfincione di patate, salsicce, ricotta e salvia

Fresh ricotta gives the filling of this thin double-crust pizza a creaminess – in contrast to the rich salty sausage. In Sicily it is called sfincione. We make these in an old wood-fired oven that was used to make bread for all the farm workers at La Gurra – the Ravidà family farm in Menfi, Sicily. It is always a day to remember – everyone is so proud of their own pizza.

MAKES 1 X 30CM/12IN DOUBLE-CRUST PIZZA

1 quantity basic pizza dough (see page 150)
2 tablespoons olive oil, plus extra for brushing
1 medium potato, finely diced
1 onion, finely sliced
1 teaspoon dried oregano
250g/9oz fresh Italian sausage, skinned
125g/4½oz fresh ricotta, crumbled
2 tablespoons chopped fresh sage
2 tablespoons freshly grated Parmesan
salt and freshly ground black pepper

1 First prepare one quantity of pizza dough (see recipe).
2 Heat the oil in a frying pan and add the potato and onion. Cook for 3–4 minutes until the onion starts to colour, and stir in the oregano. Transfer to a bowl. Fry the sausage briefly, breaking it up.
3 Knock back the dough and divide in two. Roll each piece into a thin 30cm/12in circle. Slide one circle on to a well-floured baking sheet. Spoon the potato and onion mixture on to this circle, spreading not

quite to the edges. Dot with the sausage, cover with the ricotta and sage and season.
4 Brush the edge with water and lay the remaining circle on top. Pinch and roll the edges to seal. Brush with olive oil and sprinkle with Parmesan. Make 2 or 3 holes in the pizza.
5 Bake in a preheated oven at 240°C/ 475°F/Gas 9 for 20 minutes until golden and crisp. Leave aside for about 5 minutes before serving to the let the flavours come out a little.

Tuscan bread and tomato salad

Panzanella [v]

STEPHANIE ALEXANDER shares her recipe for this essential Tuscan salad that is deliciously refreshing when made carefully. It needs a light touch with the water, and may look simple, but it is quite difficult to get the right balance!

SERVES 4

2 thick slices coarse bread, at least a day old
cold water
6 very ripe tomatoes, cubed
1 small red onion, finely chopped or very
    thinly sliced
½ cucumber, diced
1 stick celery, finely sliced
2 cloves garlic, crushed or chopped
20g/¾oz/½ cup basil leaves, torn
75ml/2½fl oz/⅓ cup extra virgin olive oil
2 tablespoons red wine vinegar
salt and freshly ground black pepper

I ordered panzanella *at Ristorante Nello La Taverna in Siena to see how a true Tuscan put it together. I was pleased to find that, with more crumbling of the bread, my version was fine. This restaurant was quite exceptional – we particularly enjoyed fresh anchovies, marinated in extra virgin olive oil, with shaved white truffles, and a torta of chickpeas and fresh artichokes. The owner told us of his philosophy regarding produce, of letting ingredients speak for themselves, of respecting the traditions of his region and yet allowing room for a personal interpretation. He could not know that he was preaching to the converted!* Panzanella *is a traditional Tuscan dish that can be expanded easily and relies on good bread, good oil and the ripest vegetables for its flavour. Elizabeth Romer records in her book* The Tuscan Year *that in some parts of Tuscany before the tomatoes ripen,* panzanella *can simply be bread, olive oil, onion and perhaps green (new) garlic. SA*

1 Remove the crusts from the bread and cut or tear into small pieces.
2 Put the bread into a bowl and sprinkle lightly with cold water. The bread should be moist but not soggy. Work the bread a little with your fingers.

3 Add the vegetables, garlic and basil. Dress with the olive oil and vinegar, then toss very gently but well and adjust the seasoning. Allow to stand for 30 minutes, so that the flavours blend. Serve.

Black pepper biscuits

Taralli [v]

These are a type of salatini, *a hard crisp salty biscuit that you will find offered with* aperitivi *in Italy. They are native to Apulia and Basilicata, and they are cooked twice – boiled then baked, so they are also a type of* biscotti.

MAKES ABOUT 40

500g/1lb 2oz/3⅓ cups plain white
(all-purpose) flour, warmed
2 tablespoons finely crushed
black peppercorns
15g/½ oz fresh yeast, 15ml/1 tablespoon
dried active baking yeast, or 1 x 7g sachet
easy-blend yeast
120ml/4fl oz/½ cup water, warmed
3 tablespoons extra virgin olive oil, warmed
175ml/6fl oz/¾ cup dry white wine, warmed
lightly crushed black peppercorns or coarse
sea salt, for coating

1 Sift the flour into a bowl and stir in the crushed black peppercorns.
2 Crumble the fresh yeast into the warm water and whisk until dissolved. Allow to stand for 10 minutes. Stir into the flour with the warmed oil and wine. Do the same for dried active yeast. For easy-blend yeast, stir directly into the flour, then add the warm water, wine and oil.
3 Mix together with a round-bladed knife, then your hands until the dough comes together. Turn out and knead until firm, smooth and elastic. Cover and allow to rest for 5 minutes.
4 Pull off a piece of dough and roll into a 5mm/¼in thick rope. Cut this into 5 cm/2in lengths and bend the ends

together to form a ring, overlapping them and pressing them together. Place on a lightly floured tea cloth. Repeat until all the dough is used up.
5 Bring a large pan of salted water to the boil. Drop the *taralli* into the water and scoop out when they rise to the surface. Drain on a clean tea towel. Dip in crushed black pepper or sea salt, shaking off the excess. Arrange on an oiled baking tray (sheet) and bake in a preheated oven at 190°C/375°F/Gas 5 for 15–20 minutes until pale golden. Transfer to a wire rack to cool. Keep in an airtight tin.

VARIATION: Add fennel seeds instead of the black pepper.

Sicilian semolina (durum) flour bread with sesame seeds

Mafalda [v]

Mafalda is the type of bread we eat in Menfi, western Sicily where I teach. It has a gorgeous yellow crumb and a deep golden crunchy exterior crust, liberally sprinkled with sesame seeds. We sometimes bake this bread in the old wood-fired oven at the local farmhouse. The bread is shaped somewhat like a firecracker – a zigzag shape with a tail lying across the middle. The sesame seeds, and probably the shape too, were brought to Sicily by the Arabs in the ninth century. Sicilian semolina (durum) flour (farina di semola) *is very fine and can be found in Italian delicatessens. If you are unable to find it, you could use coarser semolina (durum) flour by grinding it very finely in a food processor or blender. Unbleached durum wheat flour can also be used.*

MAKES 2 LOAVES

25g/1oz fresh yeast/2½ teaspoons active dry
    yeast or 2 x 7g sachet easy-blend yeast
50ml/2fl oz/¼ cup warm water
1 tablespoon olive oil
1 tablespoon malt syrup (extract)
250ml/8fl oz/1 cup water at
    room temperature
500g/1lb 2oz/3⅓ cups fine semolina
    (durum) flour
2–3 teaspoons salt
3 tablespoons sesame seeds

1 Dissolve the yeast in the warm water in a large mixing bowl. Let it stand until creamy, about 10 minutes. Whisk in the oil, malt and water.

2 In a large bowl, mix the flour with the salt and add the yeast mixture. Mix together, then bring the dough together with your hands.

3 Tip out on to a floured surface and begin to knead. The dough should be quite soft – if not add more water. Knead vigorously for 10 minutes until the dough is smooth and elastic. This develops the gluten which makes the dough stretch. It helps if you have warm hands!

4 Place the dough in a lightly oiled bowl, cover tightly with cling film (plastic wrap), and leave to rise in a warm place until doubled, about 1½ hours. The dough should be puffy.

5 Punch the dough down, knead it briefly, then cover it and let it rest for 5 minutes.

Roll it into a long, fairly narrow sausage, about 60cm/24in long. Cut the dough in half and roll each as long as you can. Starting at one end zigzag the rope against itself, leaving a tail long enough to lay lengthways over the loaf and tuck the end under.

6 Place the loaves on floured baking tray (sheet). Brush the entire surface of each loaf lightly with water and sprinkle with sesame seeds. Cover with an upturned bowl, and let rise until doubled in size, about 1–1½ hours.

7 Thirty minutes before baking, heat the oven to 220°C/425°F/Gas 7 and place a tray of hot water in the base of the oven to create steam which will help form a good crust. Bake the loaves for 10 minutes. Reduce the heat to 200°C/400°F/Gas 6 and bake 25 to 30 minutes longer. The bread is cooked when it sounds hollow when tapped on the base. Cool on racks.

Sardinian 'broken' bread

Pane frattau [V]

GIULIANO BUGIALLI introduces us to the paper-thin dry bread of Sardinia here and shows how to prepare it in the most delicious way. It is simple, but a meal fit for a king! The sheets of *carta da musica* ('music paper') bread can be found in some supermarkets or delicatessens, and are a speciality from Sardinia. They are unleavened sheets of bread and are so thin and fragile that they are said to look like old sheet music, hence their nickname.

SERVES 4

FOR THE SAUCE:

750g/1lb 10oz fresh ripe tomatoes or drained
   canned Italian tomatoes
2 tablespoons olive oil
small clove garlic, cut into slivers
a few large fresh basil leaves
salt and freshly ground black pepper

4 'sheets' *pane carasau* or *carta da
   musica* bread
1 litre/1¾ pints/4 cups vegetable or chicken
   stock (broth), preferably home-made (see
   page 49)
1 tablespoon red wine vinegar
4 extra-large eggs
freshly grated pecorino sardo or pecorino
   (romano), to serve

This is one of the most outstanding dishes made from the foods that are available to Sardinian shepherds – bread, water or stock (broth), tomatoes, local eggs and pecorino (romano) cheese. And when carefully prepared, it is simply delicious. Pane frattau *is sometimes topped with a fried egg. GB*

1 To make the sauce, roughly chop the tomatoes, then place in a medium-sized saucepan with the olive oil, garlic, basil leaves and salt and pepper to taste, and simmer for 15 minutes.

2 Pass the contents of the pan through a food mill (mouli-legumes), using the disc with the smallest holes, into a bowl. Return the strained sauce to the saucepan and reduce for 5 minutes. Check the seasoning and keep warm.

3 Set the *pane carasau (carta da musica)* bread, 1 sheet at a time, on individual plates, pour ¼ cup of the broth over each piece of bread and let soak for 5 minutes.

4 Pour a quarter of the warm tomato sauce over each sheet and spread it out with a ladle. Fold the overhanging pieces of the bread inwards to match the shape of the dish itself. Follow this procedure with all 4 sheets of bread.

5 Place a medium-sized saucepan with 700ml/1¼ pints/3 cups of cold water over medium heat. When the water comes to the boil add the wine vinegar. Break 1 egg in the water and carefully, using a small spoon, fold the white over the egg yolk; simmer for 3 minutes. Using a slotted spoon, transfer the *uovo in camicia* (poached egg) on to the bread and tomato sauce of one of the dishes. Repeat the same procedure with the other 3 eggs. Sprinkle abundant grated Parmesan over the 4 portions and serve.

Folded parsley pizza

Calzone di prezzemolo [v]

URSULA FERRIGNO presents another type of pizza here. This time it is made in the *pizzaiolo* fashion, by mixing the yeast and water straight into the flour, so that a *biga* is not used (this is a type of formented yeast starter – see *Stromboli* recipe on page 162). The dough is folded over the filling and sealed to form a half-moon shape. The parsley filling is very unusual and makes a change from the ubiquitous basil.

SERVES 2–4 AS A SNACK

7g/¼oz fresh yeast
a little caster (superfine) sugar
225–250ml/8fl oz/1 cup hand hot water
550g/1lb 4oz/3⅔ cups strong white
    unbleached (all-purpose) flour
15g/½oz/½ tablespoon salt
80–120ml/3–4fl oz olive oil
1 onion, peeled and finely chopped
a very large handful of fresh flat leaf
    parsley, chopped
350g/12oz mozzarella, cut into
    small cubes
freshly ground black pepper
plain (all-purpose) flour, for dusting

I first tasted this in Cassibile in Sicily, where it was baked in a wood-fired oven. The simple flavours of the parsley and cheese really sing out in the crisp pizza crust. The word calzone *means 'trouser leg', as this is said to resemble one! UF*

1 Cream the yeast with the sugar and a little of the water. Mix the flour and salt in a large bowl. Add half the oil and the creamed yeast with the remaining water. Mix with a wooden spoon to a dough.
2 Turn out of the bowl and knead vigorously for 10 minutes until soft and pliable. Return the soft dough to a clean bowl. Cover, and allow to rise until doubled in size for about 1 hour.
3 Meanwhile, prepare the filling by heating the remaining olive oil in a frying pan. Fry the onion until soft, then add the parsley and stir for 2 minutes over a medium heat. Season with pepper leave to one side. Mix in the cheese when cool.

4 Preheat the oven to 200°C/400°F/Gas 6. Knock back the dough and knead for 4 minutes. Roll out into a large rectangle 38 x 20cm/15 x 8in. Spread the onion and cheese mixture over the dough, leaving a 1cm/½in margin all round. Now fold the dough lengthways into three, enclosing the filling and place on a greased tray. Leave for 10 minutes to rise again and then dust with extra plain flour.
5 Bake in the oven for 20 minutes until light and golden. Cool on a wire rack and then cut into thick or thin slices for snacks or canapés. Good hot, cold or warm.

Italian flatbreads

Piadine [v]

STEPHANIE ALEXANDER cooks these well-renowned breads – one of the few non-leavened breads in Italy – at a moment's notice at her cooking course in Tuscany. This recipe originates from Romagna.

MAKES ABOUT 20

500g/1lb 2oz/3½ cups plain
   (all-purpose) flour
25g/1oz/2 tablespoons butter
salt
tepid water

These flatbreads are different from focaccia *and the bread used for* bruschetta *as they don't include a leavening agent. A* piadina *is correctly cooked on a thick flat piece of terracotta, known as a* testa. *A soaked shallow terracotta saucer intended for a fat flowerpot makes a perfect* testa, *as does an unglazed terracotta floor tile. While neither should be oiled before use, both need to be heated in a low oven or over a low flame before being used as a baking stone – this 'seasons' the* testa, *ensuring it won't crack when the* piadini *are cooking.* Piadina *dough is similar to the dough used to make* roti *in Indian cookery. Indian cooks often use half wholemeal flour and half plain (all-purpose) flour, and they serve* roti *with curries. It is always fascinating to discover similarities of technique in widely differing cultures. I tried baking the thin and very soft discs of dough in the oven on hot bricks in lieu of a* testa, *but had far better results cooking them on a hot grill (broiler) or ridged griddle for a few minutes a side until crisp with burnt, bubbly bits. I kept the* piadine *warm between a folded tea towel in a basket until all were ready.* Piadine *are ideal with antipasti (especially soft cheeses). SA*

1 Sift the flour into a basin. Make a well in the flour. Barely melt the butter, then add it to the flour with just enough lightly salted tepid water (about 200ml/7fl oz/scant 1cup) to make a dough. Knead well for 10 minutes, then wrap the dough in a cloth and put an upturned bowl over it. Leave for 30 minutes.
2 Break off about 20 pieces of dough the size of a small egg and roll each into a 5mm/¼in thick disc that is 10–12cm/4–4½in wide.

3 Heat a *testa* or heavy-based frying pan or ridged grill pan over coals or on top of the stove. Cook a disc of dough on the *testa* or pan for 3 minutes, then turn it over and cook for a further few minutes. The *piadina* will have developed slightly burned bubbles, again just like a *roti*. Keep the cooked *piadine* warm in a cloth or loosely wrapped in aluminium foil while finishing the rest. They are best served hot.

Focaccia

Focaccia [V]

Focaccia *literally means a bread baked on the hearth, but is easily baked in conventional ovens. It is found all over Italy in many different forms, and can be thin and crisp or thick and soft, or round or square. This one is made in a tin (pan) – it can be shaped on a baking tray (sheet) to any shape you wish. A terracotta bakestone (*testa*) or unglazed terracotta floor tile, heated in the oven, will give pizzas and* focaccia *extra lift and a crisp base. Although* focaccia *can be made with any basic pizza dough, the secret of a truly light* focaccia *lies in three risings, and dimpling the dough so that it traps olive oil while it bakes.*

SERVES 4–6

750g/1lb 10oz/5 cups Italian '00' flour or
   plain white (all-purpose) flour, plus extra
½ teaspoon fine salt
25g/1oz fresh yeast (for dried yeast, follow
   manufacturer's instructions)
150ml/¼ pint/⅔ cup extra virgin olive oil
450ml/16fl oz/2 cups hand-hot water
coarse sea or crystal salt
4 fresh rosemary sprigs

1 Sift the flour with the salt into a large bowl and make a well in the centre. Crumble in the yeast and pour in about 3 tablespoons olive oil, then rub in the yeast until the mixture resembles fine breadcrumbs. Pour in the water and mix together with your hands to make a dough.

2 Tip the dough out on to a floured surface, wash and dry your hands and knead for 10 minutes until smooth and elastic. The dough should be quite soft, but if too soft to handle, add more flour.

3 Place in a clean oiled bowl, cover with a damp tea towel and leave to rise in a warm place until doubled – about 1½ hours.

4 Lightly oil two shallow 25cm/10in cake tins, pie or pizza plates. Knock or punch down the dough and divide in two. Shape each into a ball on a floured surface and roll out into two 25cm/10 in circles. Place in the tins, cover with a damp tea towel and leave to rise for 30 minutes.

5 Remove the tea towel and, using your finger tips, make dimples all over the surface of the dough. They can be quite deep. Drizzle over the remaining oil and sprinkle generously with salt. Cover again and leave to rise for 30 minutes.

6 Spray with water, scatter the rosemary on top, and bake at 200°C/400°F/Gas 6 for 20–25 minutes. Transfer to a wire rack to cool. Eat the same day or freeze for another occasion – wrap in cling film (plastic wrap), freeze then thaw at room temperature for 30 minutes and reheat in a hot oven for 5 minutes to serve.

VARIATION: FIG AND PANCETTA FOCACCIA
Make up the dough as before but roll out to line a swiss roll tin (pan). Cover and allow to rise for 30 minutes. Dimple the dough as above, scatter with 5 quartered figs and 75g/3oz chopped pancetta, drizzle with the oil. Bake as above.

Pizza roll with rocket pesto and mozzarella

Stromboli con pesto di rucola e mozzarella [v]

URSULA FERRIGNO, an expert baker, introduces us to the *biga* or 'starter' method used in much Italian baking. It gives the dough a kick-start and a subtle yeasty flavour.

SERVES 2–4

FOR THE *BIGA* (STARTER):

2.5g/¹⁄₁₀ oz fresh yeast

150ml/¼ pint/²⁄₃ cup warm water
   (blood temperature)

125g/4½ oz/scant 1 cup strong (bread) flour

FOR THE DOUGH:

10g/3⅓ oz fresh yeast

175ml/6fl oz warm water
   (blood temperature)

1½ teaspoons salt

375g/13oz/2¼ cups strong (bread) flour

3 tablespoons olive oil

FOR THE ROCKET PESTO:

3 tablespoons pine nuts, toasted

2–3 cloves garlic

finely grated rind (zest) of 1 lemon

100g/4oz bunch rocket (arugula)

about 100ml/3½ fl oz olive oil, plus extra

50g/2oz/²⁄₃ cup finely grated Parmesan

300g/10oz mozzarella

salt and freshly ground black pepper

sea salt, to garnish

fresh rosemary sprigs, to garnish

This is an interesting shape of pizza, rolled up like a swiss roll around a pesto made with rocket (arugula) and filled with stringy melting mozzarella. A biga starter gives a nice chewy texture and an almost sourdough flavour. UF

1 Preheat oven to 200°C/400°F/Gas 6. To make the *biga*, dissolve the fresh yeast in the water. Add the flour and mix to a smooth, thick batter. Cover and leave to ferment at room temperature for 12–36 hours until loose and bubbling.

2 To make the dough, dissolve the fresh yeast in half of the water. In a large bowl, mix the salt into the flour – make a well in the centre. Pour in the yeast mixture, olive oil and *biga* and combine. Add remaining water and mix to form a soft, sticky dough, adding extra water if necessary.

3 Turn out on to a floured surface and knead until silky and elastic, about 10 minutes. Place dough in a clean oiled bowl, cover and leave to rise until doubled in size, about 1½–2 hours.

4 Make the pesto. Process the pine nuts and garlic until finely chopped in a food processor. Add the lemon rind (zest), rocket (arugula) and one-third of the olive oil and process until the required texture is achieved, gradually adding more olive oil. Stir in the Parmesan by hand and season with salt. Adjust the olive oil content, to reach desired consistency – this pesto needs to be quite thick.

5 Knock back and chafe (a rotating, shaping motion), then rest for 10 minutes. Roll out into a rectangle approximately 35 x 20cm/14 x 8in. Slice the mozzarella thinly and lay evenly over the dough. Smother in the rocket pesto.

6 Roll the dough like a swiss roll, starting at one of the shorter sides. Do not roll too tightly. Place on an oiled baking tray (sheet) and pierce the rolled dough in several places with a knife or skewer. Sprinkle with olive oil, sea salt and rosemary. Bake in a preheated oven for about 1 hour or until golden brown.

7 Remove from the oven, cool slightly then and sprinkle with additional olive oil.

10

Desserts,
Cakes and
Biscuits

Walnut tart from Val d'Aosta

Torta di noci d'Aosta

CARLA TOMASI presents a rare recipe for a pastry and walnut tart, which is typical of the cooking in the north.

MAKES ONE 25CM/10IN CAKE

FOR THE FILLING:
350g/12oz/1²/₃ cups granulated sugar
6 tablespoons of cold water
350g/12oz/3 cups just-shelled walnuts (shelled weight), coarsely chopped by hand
120ml/4fl oz/¾ cup double (heavy) cream at room temperature

FOR THE PASTRY:
350g/12oz/2½ cups '00' grade Italian flour
150g/5oz/²/₃ cup caster (superfine) sugar
pinch fine sea salt
200g/7oz/scant 1 cup unsalted (sweet) butter, cut into dice and thoroughly chilled
1 whole egg
1 egg yolk
2 or 3 tablespoons iced water – if necessary

This wonderful cake should be made during the winter months when nuts of any type are at their best. This is classified as a dolce da tè *(cake for tea) and therefore never served after a meal as a dessert. However it can be served late in the morning with an espresso or at teatime. Make the filling with* just-*shelled walnuts, as they turn rancid quickly. Chill all the ingredients and utensils before making pastry for the best results. CT*

1 Place the sugar in a thick-bottomed, shallow saucepan, not much smaller than 25cm/10in in diameter. Moisten the sugar with the water and gently stir it around. Place it on a low flame and let it dissolve slowly. If sugar crystals start to burn around the sides take a pastry brush, dip it in cold water and wash them down into the rest of the sugar. Make sure all the sugar has dissolved before reaching any of the caramel stages. Failure to do so will turn the melted sugar into crystals.

2 Cook the sugar till pale yellow, draw the pan off the heat and add the walnuts. Stir a couple of times and then add the cream. Make sure the cream is at room temperature – any colder and it will set the walnut caramel into a hard mass. To melt the caramel you will have to cook it again (without being protected by the pastry layers) and by doing so, you could brown the walnuts too much and impart a bitter burnt flavour. Once the cream has been added you might help the mixture to loosen by throwing in a few tablespoons of scalding water. Leave the caramel to cool down completely before using or it will spoil the pastry.

3 Place the flour, the sugar and the salt into the well-chilled bowl of the food processor. Pulse a dozen times, then add the butter and pulse again until well incorporated into the flour. Drop in the whole egg and the yolk and pulse again a dozen times. Take the lid off and feel the mixture – be careful not to touch the blades– and if too sandy add a little water and carry on pulsing, until a pastry ball just forms on top of the blades. Scoop the 'loose' pastry on the worktop and knead it a couple of times– do not let the butter melt on to your hands. If the pastry is cool enough you could roll it straight away– as long as you are quite quick. If not leave it to chill until ready to handle.

4 Divide the pastry into two, one piece smaller than the other. Roll out the larger piece quite thinly to fit the bottom and side of a 25cm/10in tart tin. Spoon in the walnut filling and cover with the remaining rolled-out pastry. Seal the edges, brush the top with cold water and dust with caster sugar. Bake in a preheated oven at 180°C/350°F/Gas 4 for 30–40 minutes, until the pastry is a rich biscuit colour. A few minutes after the pie has been taken out of the oven, check for any sugary filling that may have escaped. As soon as it is possible take the pie out of the tin and leave to cool on a wire rack.

To help you slide the pie from the base of the tin on to the rack, run a long palette knife under the base. Do not let the pie cool inside the tin, as moisture will certainly form beneath and the result will be a spongy bottom crust.

CLAUDIO PECORARI

Sweet plum gnocchi

Gnocchi de susine

CLAUDIO PECORARI, who makes the best savoury potato *gnocchi*, includes here this sweet version. They are quite common in his native region of Friuli-Venezia Giulia. Incidentally, the *Polonese dolce* garnish is a classic Italian sweet recipe. A savoury Polonese garnish involves finely chopped egg white, sieved egg yolks and fried breadcrumbs, while the sweet version as shown here has just the buttery fried breadcrumbs. It's origins lie in Polish cuisine.

SERVES 4

1 quantity potato *gnocchi* (see page 82)
8 fresh blue plums or 12 prunes
caster (superfine) sugar (or jam, see method)

FOR THE *POLONESE DOLCE* GARNISH:
100g/4oz/8 tablespoons butter
3 tablespoons fresh white breadcrumbs
ground cinnamon, for dusting

Gnocchi de susine or plum gnocchi *were often made at home for my brother and I. Our mother use to stuff the dough with juicy blue plums. After she had split them almost in half to take out the stone, she put in some jam. She closed them and cleverly wrapped them in* gnocchi *dough. Then she would boil and drain them and sprinkle them with sugar and cinnamon, keeping them warm on the stove with a little melted butter – one of my favourite childhood memories! The crunchiness of the* Polonese dolce *garnish is a fantastic contrast to the soft* gnocchi *dough and the luscious melting plum filling. It is very sensual! For each person you will require 3 prunes or 2 fresh blue plums. Remember that for each of the prunes or plums, you will need the same amount of* gnocchi *dough or slightly more. CP*

1 Prepare the potato *gnocchi* following the recipe provided.
2 If working with prunes soak them in warm water until they swell. If working with fresh plums, blanch them in hot simmering water until you can prise them open to remove the stone.
3 Open the plums or prunes and place a half teaspoon of sugar where the stone was, or as I prefer, a teaspoon of apricot jam laced with Maraschino. Close them and pull off a similar size piece of dough.
4 Make a well in the dough and place the prune or plum in it. Carefully wrap the dough around it and seal. Roll the *gnocchi* in your palm. Rest on a floured tea towel.

5 Put a large pan of water on to boil. When boiling, add a touch of salt and plunge the *gnocchi* in. They are cooked when they rise to the surface.
6 In the meantime, to make the *Polonese dolce* garnish, melt the butter and when foamy add the fresh breadcrumbs toasting them slightly until crisp.
7 Rescue the *gnocchi* from the boiling water, where they will be floating, and put them on the serving plate. Pour or sprinkle the breadcrumbs on to the *gnocchi* and add a dusting of cinnamon.

Lemon and chocolate roll

Dolce di limone e cioccolato

FRANCESCA ROMINA's recipe for this lemon roll cake with chocolate is quite simply superb! Lemons are made into a curd and used to fill the centre of a sweet paste roll with chocolate pieces. Very delicious!

MAKES 2 MEDIUM/SMALL CAKES

FOR THE LEMON FILLING:
6 large egg yolks
200g/7oz/1cup caster (superfine) sugar
120ml/4fl oz/½ cup freshly squeezed
    lemon juice
1 teaspoon lemon-flavoured liqueur (optional)
¼ teaspoon vanilla essence (extract)
50g/2oz/¼ cup unsalted butter, cut into
    small pieces

FOR THE DOUGH:
3 eggs
100g/3½oz/½ cup caster (superfine) sugar
¾ teaspoon vanilla essence (extract)
350g/12oz/2½ cups plain white
    (all-purpose) flour
2 teaspoons baking powder
100g/3½oz/½ cup pure lard (solid
    vegetable shortening)
½ teaspoon ground cinnamon
350g /12oz/1½ cups dark chocolate, cut into
    small pieces
75g/2½oz/½ cup flaked (sliced) almonds
icing sugar (confectioner's sugar),
    for sprinkling

This recipe was given to my grandmother by a relative from Ciminna, Sicily. It is an unusual cake in that it can be eaten warm or cold. For those who go crazy over lemon roll cake, this recipe is for you. It can be made on the spur of the moment, and the lemon filling can be the one included here, the one from your favourite lemon meringue pie recipe, a purchased lemon pie filling or lemon curd. (You will need two 450g/1lb cans or jars.) Since this recipe yields two cakes, you can make it for large gatherings or give one cake away to friends or relatives. Wrapped in foil, these cakes will keep for about a week in the refrigerator. FR

1 To make the lemon filling: In the top pan of a medium-size double boiler, combine the egg yolks and sugar. Place over (not touching) gently simmering water in the bottom pan and cook, stirring constantly, until just combined about 2 minutes. Stir in the lemon juice, liqueur (if using), and vanilla. Continue to stir over gently simmering water until the curd thickens and coats the back of the spoon, about 10 minutes. Add the butter one piece at a time, stirring until melted before adding the next piece. Remove from heat and let cool to room temperature. (If not using immediately, transfer to a sterilized jar, cover tightly, and refrigerate for up to 1 week.)

2 To make the dough, beat together the eggs, sugar, and vanilla in a small bowl. Set aside.

3 On a work surface, sift together the flour and baking powder. Add the lard (vegetable shortening), breaking it up with your hands until the mixture resembles little peas. Make a well in the centre. Using a fork, slowly mix in the egg mixture until a dough forms. Knead until smooth, about 3 minutes. Cover with a damp kitchen towel and leave to rest on the work surface for 15 minutes.

4 Preheat an oven to 190°C/375°F/Gas 5. On a well-floured work surface, cut the dough in half. Roll out each half into a 23 x 25cm/9 x 10in rectangle. Transfer the rectangles to a large, buttered baking tray (sheet). Spoon half of the lemon filling lengthways down the centre of each rectangle, forming a strip. Then sprinkle each strip of lemon filling with half the cinnamon, half the chocolate, and 2 tablespoons of the sliced almonds. To form each roll, fold in the sides so they overlap. With your thumb, press together edges of dough at each end to seal.

5 Bake until the tops and bottoms are golden brown, about 35 minutes. (If the cakes are golden brown on the bottom and done, but the tops aren't browned, place them under a preheated grill (broiler) for just a few seconds to brown.) Allow the cakes to cool for 15 minutes on the baking sheet, then sprinkle with the remaining almond slices, icing (confectioner's) sugar, and a little cinnamon. Serve warm.

TIP: Make sure to seal the edges of the cake well or the filling will slip out during baking. Sometimes it splits – don't worry, it will taste just as good!

Chestnut cake with little pears and mild Gorgonzola

Torta di castagne con perine e Gorgonzola dolce

I make this in Tuscany where they celebrate the beginning of the chestnut season with sagras *or local festivals where roasted chestnuts are munched with copious amounts of new wine! This cake is a type of genoese or whisked sponge made with chestnut flour and is very light and moist. Served with rich and runny* Gorgonzola dolce *and the little pears always in season in October, it is a triumph!*

SERVES 8

175g/6oz/12 tablespoons butter, plus extra
   for greasing
3 eggs
175g/6oz/¾ cup caster (superfine) sugar
175g/6oz/1¼ cups chestnut flour (*farina di
   castagne*), sifted twice
5 tablespoons *vin santo* or Marsala

TO SERVE:
8 ripe baby pears (*perine*), or 4 pears, halved
350g/12oz Gorgonzola dolce (dolcelatte), left
   out at room temperature overnight so that it
   is really runny!

1 Preheat the oven to 180°C/350°F/Gas 4. Butter and flour a 23cm/9in spring-form tin (pan) then line the base with greased and floured greaseproof (waxed) paper.
2 Melt the butter and set aside to cool slightly. Beat the eggs until pale and creamy. Gradually whisk in the sugar and continue whisking until the mixture thickens, doubles in bulk and forms a ribbon trail when the whisk is lifted. It is now ready.
3 Using a large metal spoon, carefully fold in the chestnut flour, then the butter and finally the wine. Do not overfold or the cake will not rise.

4 Spoon the mixture carefully into the prepared tin (pan). Bake in the preheated oven for about 35–45 minutes. Test after 35 minutes. The cake should look well-risen, light brown and slightly shrunk from the edges. The top should be springy, the crumb moist.
5 Turn the cake out on to a wire cake rack to cool, then remove the paper. Place the cake in an airtight container until ready to serve. It is better cooked the day before and left to mature. Dust the top with icing sugar and serve cut into thin slices, each with a small pear and a spoonful of runny Gorgonzola dolce.

Coffee pannacotta 'drowned' in coffee sauce

Panna cotta al caffè 'affogato'

Pannacotta is literally cooked cream, set with gelatine, but you can add all sorts of flavourings to the basic mix. It should be barely set – so it just wobbles. Originally this comes form the north, where the first rich thick cream was skimmed off the milk and set on its own. Leaf gelatine is used here as it is easier to handle than in its powdered form.

SERVES 4–6

600ml/1 pint/2 $\frac{1}{2}$ cups double (heavy) cream
125g/4 $\frac{1}{2}$ oz/ $\frac{1}{2}$ cup caster (superfine) sugar
3 teaspoons instant espresso coffee granules
1 vanilla pod, split
7g/1 sheet leaf gelatine (1 tablespoon gelatin)
4 tablespoons milk

FOR THE COFFEE SYRUP:
250ml/8fl oz/1 cup cold espresso coffee
125g/4 $\frac{1}{2}$ oz/ $\frac{1}{2}$ cup granulated sugar
3 tablespoons coffee liqueur

1 Lightly oil 4–6 ramekins or moulds. Heat the cream, sugar, coffee and vanilla pod until almost but not boiling, stirring occasionally. Leave to infuse for about 20 minutes. Whisk to dissolve the coffee.
2 Soak the leaf gelatine in warm water until soft then drain. Pour the milk into a small pan and heat slowly. When warm, stir in the gelatine until dissolved.
3 Stir this into the coffee cream mixture. Bring to the boil, then immediately take off the heat and strain into a jug. Pour the hot cream into the oiled ramekins. Cool then chill in the refrigerator for several hours or until set.
4 To make the coffee syrup, put the espresso coffee into a pan with the sugar and heat gently, stirring until the sugar is dissolved. Cool, then stir in the liqueur.
5 Carefully loosen the creams and turn out on to individual plates. Serve the syrup in a jug to pour over the cream.

Chocolate, hazelnut and cherry cake

Torta di gianduja con ciliege

'Gianduja' is a mixture of chocolate and hazelnuts, very popular in Piedmont. Serve this in thin slices – it is very rich and moist. The cherries may sink to the bottom, but this doesn't matter at all. It is wonderful dessert when served with some cool mascarpone.

SERVES 6–8

150g/5oz/10 tablespoons unsalted (sweet)
   butter, softened
125g/4 $\frac{1}{2}$ oz/ $\frac{1}{2}$ cup caster (superfine) sugar
flour, for dusting
4 eggs, separated
finely grated rind (zest) of 1 lemon
6 tablespoons fine dry brown breadcrumbs
150g/5oz/1 cup blanched hazelnuts
125g/4 $\frac{1}{2}$ oz dark (semi-sweet) chocolate, grated
225g/8oz fresh cherries, stoned

1 Preheat the oven to 170°C/325°F/Gas 3. Brush a 23 cm/9in springform cake tin (pan) with melted butter, allow to set, then dust out with flour. Line the base with non-stick baking parchment.
2 In a bowl, cream the butter with $\frac{2}{3}$ of the sugar until pale and creamy. Beat in the egg yolks, one at a time, then the lemon rind (zest) and breadcrumbs.
3 Finely (and quickly) grind the hazelnuts in a blender or food processor. Fold into the egg mixture with the grated chocolate.
4 In another bowl, whisk the egg whites until stiff but not dry. Whisk in the remaining sugar, until stiff and shiny. Gently fold into the cake mixture. Finally, fold in the cherries.
5 Carefully spoon into the cake tin (pan), level the surface and bake for about 1 hour until risen and firm to the touch. To test, insert a skewer into the middle – it should come out clean. Remove from tin (pan) and cool on a wire rack. Serve with a good blob of mascarpone.

Sienese almond biscuits (cookies)

Ricciarelli

JUDY WITTS FRANCINI's perfect biscuits (cookies) are crisp on the outside and soft inside.

These delicate Christmas cookies are said to be shaped like the almond eyes of the Madonna in Renaissance paintings. They originate from Siena. JWF

MAKES ABOUT 16 BISCUITS (COOKIES)

175g/6oz blanched almonds, ground
1 tablespoon plain (all-purpose) flour
½ teaspoon baking powder
200g/7oz/scant 1 cup caster
    (superfine) sugar, plus extra for rolling in
2 large egg whites
3 drops almond essence (extract)

1 Preheat the oven to 200°C/400°F/Gas 6. Grind the almonds in a blender and place in a bowl with the sugar. Mix the baking powder with the flour and fold into the almonds. Beat the egg whites until stiff and stir into the mixture. Add the almond extract and blend until a soft paste.
2 Sprinkle some caster (superfine) sugar on a clean, dry surface. Form one tablespoon of dough into a small ball, roll in the sugar, and shape into the traditional diamond shape by rolling into a sausage and tapering the ends. Flatten the biscuit (cookie) with the palm of your hand.
3 Place the cookies on a baking tray (sheet) covered with non-stick baking parchment. Bake for 10–12 minutes until lightly golden.

'Peppered' spice cake from Siena

Panpepato

This rich, fruit honey and nut packed disc-like 'cake' is served in thin slices after dinner or with coffee. It originates in Siena, where every confectioner's shop has their own variation, and people are known to pilgrimage there just for panforte, *a similar spice cake.*

MAKES ONE 20.5CM/8IN CAKE

100g/4oz walnut halves
100g/4oz whole skinned hazelnuts
100g/4oz candied orange peel
100g/4oz candied citron peel
50g/2oz dried figs, chopped
50g/2oz/scant ½ cup plain white
    (all-purpose) flour
3 tablespoons cocoa powder
¼ teaspoon each ground coriander, black
    pepper, nutmeg, cloves and cinnamon
100g/4oz/½ cup granulated sugar
225g/8oz runny honey
25g/1oz/2 tablespoons butter
icing (confectioner's) sugar, to dust

1 Grease and line a 20.5cm/8in spring-form tin (pan) with non-stick baking parchment or edible rice paper. Spread the walnuts and hazelnuts on a baking tray (sheet) and bake in the oven at 180°C/350°F/Gas 4 for 10–15 minutes until golden brown. Cool slightly, chop roughly and place in a medium bowl.
2 Turn the oven down to 150°C/300°F/Gas 2. Chop the orange and citron peel finely and stir into the nuts with the figs, flour, cocoa and spices.
3 Put the sugar, honey, and butter in a saucepan and heat gently, stirring occasionally until dissolved. Bring to the boil and boil until the syrup reaches the soft ball stage (242°F–248°F) on a sugar thermometer. Quickly stir in the nut mixture and pour into the prepared tin (pan). Smooth the surface with an oiled potato masher. Work quickly or the mixture will set.
4 Bake in the oven for 35 minutes. The cake will not brown or set at this stage. Transfer to cool on a wire rack. The cake will harden as it cools. When cold, remove the tin (pan) and baking parchment (but not the rice paper) and dredge with icing (confectioner's) sugar. Serve in thin slices.

NOTE: This will keep for 1 month in an airtight tin.

Sweet aniseed biscotti

Ciambelline al vino, dalla Ciociaria

CARLA TOMASI shows us the diversity of Italian baking once again – these are biscuits (cookies), but not as we know them!

WILL MAKE ABOUT 50 *CIAMBELLINE*

200ml/7fl oz/scant 1 cup extra virgin olive oil
2 heaped tablespoons whole aniseed
1 whole egg (about 80g/3oz)
200g/7oz/1 cup caster (superfine) sugar
200ml/7fl oz/ scant 1 cup dry white wine
900g/2lb/6 cups '00' grade Italian flour,
    plus extra
2 teaspoons baking powder (double active)
2 teaspoons bicarbonate of soda
    (baking soda)
100g/4oz/½ cup granulated sugar (placed in a
    small bowl)

La Ciociaria is an area in southern Lazio (south-east of Rome) with a very ancient culinary past. Its cooking is rooted in a strong farmhouse background – la cucina del territorio – and these ciambelline are a perfect example of its sophisticated simplicity. Ciambelline are ring shaped biscuits (cookies) that, like the more famous cantucci of Tuscany, need to be dipped in wine to soften them up. They are made with extra virgin olive oil, neither peppery nor grassy in flavour, and in Central Italy you'll find them in bakeries, or at the bread counter of many delicatessens. They keep well if stored in an airtight box and are very easy to make. CT

1 Heat 2 tablespoons of the olive oil in a frying pan and lightly toast the aniseed. Leave to cool a little. Break the egg in a large bowl, add the oil and whip it up to an emulsion with an electric whisk. Add the sugar in stages, still whisking on a high speed, then the wine.

2 Sift the flour with the baking powder and soda. Put down the electric whisk, change to a wooden spoon and start adding the flour. Stir quickly but not so vigorously as to wake up too much of the gluten. The baked texture should be crumbly rather than doughy. Then pat it into a soft but not sticky loaf (add the extra flour if necessary) and turn it out of the bowl.

3 Knead it briefly and then cut in two and shape into logs. Leave to rest (to relax the gluten) well covered with cling film (plastic wrap) for 30 minutes or so. Then with a sharp knife, slice off pieces of about 25g/1oz. I suggest to weigh a few of the first pieces or until you can guess by feel. By doing so you will achieve three goals: they will all bake at the same time, they will look appealing on a plate, and they will fit easily in rows on the baking trays (sheets).

4 Roll the pieces of dough into a length of 15cm/6in and shape into rings by slightly overlapping the ends. Now pick up the rings – using your thumb and index fingers – by holding them at the joined ends and drop them upside-down into the sugar-filled bowl. Pick them up again and place them – quite close and sugar-side up – on a baking tray (sheet) lined with non-stick parchment paper. Just make sure that no more than few specks of sugar sit on the tray or it will burn underneath the *ciambelline*. They do not swell up a lot, but just plump up nicely!

5 Bake in a preheated oven at 180°C/350°F/Gas 4 for 15 minutes and then reduce to 160°C/325°F/Gas 3 and bake for a further 15 minutes or until golden brown and 'dry' to the touch. Make sure before you take them out of the oven, that they are not doughy inside, and the best way to do so is to break into one. Baking times stated vary according to the type of oven you have, so take care.

VARIATION: A nice variation is to make them with a good red wine, cinnamon in place of the aniseed and few tablespoons of dark roasted (crushed) hazelnuts.

Little pistachio cakes from Mazara del Vallo

Mazarisi

I like to serve these with sorbets and ice cream in Sicily. They are quite dry and have that unmistakable delicate pistachio flavour. Avoid adding any extra flavourings. They originate from Mazara del Vallo, a town near Menfi that still has an old medina – Arab quarter. These delicious madeleine-like cakes are also delightful served with a moscato *dessert wine.*

MAKES ABOUT 24 LITTLE CAKES

125g/4½oz/¾ cup unsalted shelled and
   peeled pistachio nuts
100g/4oz/½ cup sugar
finely grated rind (zest) of 1 orange
½ teaspoon salt
150g/5oz/¼ cup plus 2 tablespoons plain
   (all-purpose) flour
1 teaspoon potato starch or corn starch
11 egg yolks
5 egg whites
butter, for greasing

1 Preheat the oven to 160°C/325°F/Gas 3.
2 Grind the pistachios in a food processor with the sugar and pour mixture into a mixing bowl. Add the orange rind, salt, flour, and potato starch and mix well.
3 Beat in the egg yolks, one at a time, mixing gently after adding each one. Whisk the egg whites until stiff and gently fold into the batter.

4 Grease small (non-stick) oval moulds (I sometimes use tiny madeleine tins [pans]) with butter, dust with flour and fill them with the batter. Alternatively, fill little paper cases with the mixture. Bake for 25–30 minutes, or until firmly set. They shouldn't colour very much. Remove from the moulds while still warm and cool on a cake rack.

Campari and blood orange granita

Granita di tarrocchi e Campari

Granitas save the Italians from going mad in the summer heat – there is nothing better to cool you down. This is one of the most refreshing granitas I know. What a colour! If the marvellous blood oranges are not around, try using navel oranges or even clementines. Campari is so Italian. Whether it is made with soda or with fresh orange juice, it is very evocative! You can make this into a sorbet by freezing the mixture in an ice cream machine until thick, adding a lightly beaten egg white and churning until thick, but I prefer granita.

MAKES ABOUT 750ML/26FL OZ/3¼ CUPS

6–8 blood oranges to give 500ml/18fl oz/
   2¼ cups juice (or carton blood orange juice)
   and rind (zest)
100g/4oz/½ cup granulated sugar
3–4 tablespoons Campari
1 egg white (for the sorbet only)

1 Thoroughly scrub the oranges in warm soapy water, rinse and dry. Use a sharp potato peeler to remove the rind (zest) but no white pith from 2 of the oranges. Shave off any pith and chop the rind (zest).
2 Put into a food processor or blender with the sugar and process until the zest and the sugar are well-blended and the sugar looks 'damp'.
3 Squeeze the juice from all the oranges. Spoon the flavoured sugar into a large measuring jug, then add enough strained orange juice to measure 500ml/18fl oz/2¼ cups.
4 Stir in 3 tablespoons of Campari, adding a further tablespoon if not strong enough (but no more or the mixture will not freeze to the right texture). Cover and chill in the refrigerator.

5 When ready, still freeze in a shallow metal or foil container, mashing with a fork every 20 minutes to make a nice flaky granita. Serve immediately or cover and freeze for up to 2 days. Fork up before serving in chilled or frozen glasses.

VARIATION: To make a sorbet, pour in the chilled liquid into an ice cream machine and churn until it starts to thicken. Beat the egg white until just frothy pour into the sorbet with the machine still running. Continue churning until the sorbet is very firm. Serve immediately or quickly scrape into plastic freezer boxes (which have been in the freezer for 10 minutes at least) and cover with greaseproof (waxed) paper and a lid. Label and freeze. Allow to soften for 20 minutes in the refrigerator and serve.

Ricotta and orange blossom honey ice cream

Gelato di ricotta con miele dei fiori d'arance

Ice cream is so important to the Italian way of life, and I developed this recipe after tasting a ricotta ice cream in the Pasticceria Mazzara in Palermo. I have made this with still-warm ewe's milk ricotta! The orange blossom honey in Sicily is really exotic and gives a wonderful flavour to this ice cream. In general, Sicilian ice creams are not made with eggs – just milk. Make sure this one softens for 20 minutes in the refrigerator before serving.

MAKES ABOUT 1.5 LITRES/2¾ PINTS/6¾ CUPS

450g/1lb/2 cups fresh ricotta
500ml/18fl oz/2¼ cups whole milk
125g/4½oz/½ cup caster (superfine) sugar
1 cinnamon stick
1 vanilla pod, split
1 long strip orange rind (zest)
3 tablespoons orange blossom honey, plus
   extra for drizzling
orange blossom, to garnish

1 Press the ricotta through a sieve. Place in a medium saucepan and add the milk, and sugar. Stir in the cinnamon stick, vanilla pod and orange rind (zest). Bring up to the boil, remove from heat let infuse for 10 minutes.

2 Remove the vanilla pod, cinnamon stick and orange rind (zest). Stir in the honey. Pass the ice cream mixture through a fine sieve or strainer into a bowl, cool and place in the refrigerator.

3 When nicely chilled, transfer to an ice cream maker and freeze according to manufacturer's instructions. If necessary, do this in 2 batches, keeping one batch refrigerated while freezing the other. Serve straight out of the churn for luscious soft ice cream or…

4 Spoon into individual moulds or into a chilled container. Cover and freeze until for at least 4 hours until set.

5 To serve, turn out the ice cream by dipping the moulds into a bowl of warm water for about 10 seconds. Insert a thin knife halfway into the centre of the ice cream, and twist to loosen. Invert the mould on to a plate, drizzle with a little extra warm honey and decorate with orange blossom. Serve immediately.

Watermelon sorbet with chocolate chips

Sorbetto di anguria con semi di cioccolato

This is a great favourite when we make it in Sicily – so cool and refreshing! It is always made with a hint of cinnamon, and in some cases, very exotic jasmine flower water. You see this mixture in all forms, particularly in a 'jelly' (jello) form, which is not to everyone's taste! You probably won't need a whole watermelon for this recipe, so keep the rest to eat chilled on its own or make into a fruit salad.

SERVES 4–6

750g/1lb 10oz skinned, cubed watermelon
300g/10oz/1¼ cups caster (superfine) sugar
   (depending on the sweetness of
   the watermelon)
1 cinnamon stick
freshly squeezed juice of 2 lemons
a little pink food colouring (only if necessary)
1 egg white
125g/4½oz chocolate chips (drops)

1 Remove the seeds from the melon with the tip of a small knife. Liquidize the melon, then with the machine running, pour in the sugar and blend for about 30 seconds.

2 Pour the melon mixture into a saucepan and add the cinnamon stick. Slowly bring to the boil, stirring all the time to completely dissolve the sugar, then turn down the heat and barely simmer for 1 minute. Remove from the heat, add the lemon juice and cool, adding a few drops of pink food colouring (only if really necessary, if it lacks a strong pink lustre).

3 When cold, remove the cinnamon stick and chill the mixture in the refrigerator for at least 1 hour (or overnight). This makes freezing it easier later on.

4 Freeze in an ice cream maker for the best results. When half-frozen, lightly whisk the egg white and add with the machine running. Stir in the chocolate chips (drops) at the end. Place in a freezer container. Cover with non-stick baking parchment.

5 Alternatively, pour into a shallow freezer tray and freeze until the sorbet is frozen around the edges. Mash the sorbet well with a fork. Whisk the egg white until stiff. Then, using an electric hand whisk, drop spoonfuls of the sorbet into the egg white, whisking all the time until the mixture is thick and foamy, and return to the freezer to firm up. Stir in the chocolate chips (drops) when almost frozen. Freeze until solid. Allow to soften in the refrigerator for 20 minutes before serving.

The original 'panettone'

Pandolce genovese

CARLA TOMASI believes that baking should not be rushed and she's right – take your time to achieve perfection and it is worth it!

SERVES MORE THAN 10 PEOPLE

FOR THE STARTER:
300ml/10fl oz/1¼ cups lukewarm water
25g/1oz fresh yeast or 2 x 7g sachets active dried yeast
about 500g/1lb 2oz/3⅓ cups '00' grade Italian flour, or less

FOR THE DOUGH:
175g/6oz/12 tablespoons unsalted (sweet) butter, softened to the consistency of thick double cream
200g/7oz/1 cup granulated sugar
150ml/¼ pint/⅔ cup Marsala, lukewarm
rind (zest) of 1 large, washed orange
2 tablespoons of orange flower water
4 tablespoons lightly toasted fennel seeds
1 teaspoon of fine sea salt
about 400g/14oz/2¾ cups '00' grade Italian flour (plus extra to hand)
icing (confectioner's) sugar (optional)

FOR THE FILLING:
50g/2oz/½ cup pine nuts
150g/5oz/ scant cup natural or Muscatel raisins, soaked in a little hot white wine until plumped up, drained and patted dry
50g/2oz/½ cup shelled and peeled unsalted pistachio nuts
100g/4oz/⅓ cup candied orange (peel or whole fruit) chopped into small pieces
1 tablespoon ground cinnamon mixed with 1 tablespoon granulated sugar

Pandolce is the Genoese Christmas cake. Originally it was prepared for the short festive season and was made daily. Then, the taller and mass-produced version, called panettone, became dominant. Note that enriched doughs must rise for a set time to avoid a hard crust forming. CT

1 To make the 'starter', pour the water in a bowl, crumble the yeast over it and dissolve it with a balloon whisk. Change to a wooden spoon and add enough flour (most or all of it) to form a thick 'porridge'. Cover the bowl with a cloth or cling film (plastic wrap) and leave to rise until puffed up (30–50 minutes).
2 Place the starter dough in the bowl of a food mixer. Incorporate the butter, in stages, using the paddle attachment. Add the dough ingredients one by one (you may not need all the flour) and 'paddle' for a minute or so. Now change to the hook attachment and work the dough on a low speed until it looks smooth, bouncy and not at all sticky. Scoop the dough on a floured worktop and knead for a couple of minutes. Gather into a ball, give it a light dusting of flour and place in a large plastic bowl, big enough for it to treble in volume. Cover with cling film (plastic wrap)and wrap in a clean thick cloth or towel away from any direct heat to rise at its own pace (3 hours).
3 Mix all the ingredients for the filling and set aside. When the dough is ready, lightly dust a wooden work surface with flour. Scoop the dough on to the flour and gently pat it into a large round. Cover the surface of the dough with the filling ingredients. Push them in firmly so none are left on top to burn.
4 Line a deep round 25 x 5cm/10 x 2in tin (pan) with a triple layer of non-stick baking parchment. Fold the edges of the dough towards the centre and press firmly down. When all the filling is secured, flip the dough upside down and mould into a ball. Place in the tin (pan) and flatten it gently to fit to the edge. Loosely cover it with a damp cloth, to allow the dough to expand freely. Leave to rise (up to 1½–2 hours). It is ready when the dough has nearly trebled and feels springy.
5 When ready to bake, cut a triangle shape on the top with a sharp knife. Bake in a preheated oven at 180°C/350°F/Gas 4 for 40–50 minutes, rotating back-to-front every 20 minutes. It bakes to a dark mahogany colour. Store for a day before slicing.

11

Preserves,
Drinks
and Liqueurs

Candied peel

Scorzetta candita

This really is easy to do and worth it if you use a lot of peel – think of the price of buying it pre-prepared in the shops compared with how much peel you may throw away from peeling fruit! It tastes infinitely better too. Every Italian chef or cook I have talked to will not use the pre-packaged chopped peels. Candied peel is fundamental to many savoury dishes as well as desserts. In Italy, candied fruits are often sold behind the cheese and cold meats counter in supermarkets – you have to ask. It is worth it though – the selection is brought to you in the box and you can pick out your own choice, from whole mandarin oranges to little figs.

MAKES 450G/1LB

3 oranges
4 lemons or 2 grapefruit
350g/12oz/1½ cups granulated sugar

1 Wash or scrub the fruit thoroughly, halve or quarter it and remove the pulp.
2 Place the peel in a saucepan and almost cover with cold water. Bring to the boil then simmer, half-covered for 1–2 hours until tender. (Change the water 2–3 times when cooking grapefruit peel.) Lift out of the pan and drain well.
3 Make the remaining liquid up to 600ml/1 pint/2½ cups with water. Add 225g/8oz/1 cup of the sugar, dissolve over a low heat, then bring to the boil. Add the peel and leave to steep for 2 days.
4 Drain off the syrup, dissolve the remaining sugar in it, and simmer the peel in this syrup until semi-transparent. The peel can be left in this thick syrup for about 2–3 weeks.
5 Drain off the syrup and place the peel on a wire rack standing on some newspaper or a tray to dry. Put the rack in a warm place such as an airing cupboard, in the oven at the lowest setting with the door slightly ajar, or in the residual heat of the oven after cooking. The temperature should not exceed 50°C/120°F or the fruit may turn a nasty brown. The drying will take several hours, and is finished when the peel feels dry. Store in airtight jars or containers.

Almond milk

Latte di mandorla

My food-find companion Annie and I searched for the best almond milk in Sicily and found it (as Jeffrey Steingarten had mentioned in The Man Who Ate Everything), in Syracuse. Later on that day, we found the special paste to make it in a little market in the old town – it sits in my refrigerator still – I can't bear to use it! Here's how to make it at home. Use the freshest almonds you can find – using unblanched almonds will help the freshness.

MAKES ABOUT 1 LITRE/1¾ PINTS/4 CUPS

100g/4oz/1 heaped cup unblanched almonds
4 tablespoons sugar
700ml/1¼ pints/3 cups water

1 Blanch the almonds by covering them in boiling water, leaving for 5 minutes then gradually slipping them out of their skins.
2 Place them with the sugar in a blender or liquidizer and blend until finely ground. With the machine still running, gradually add the water. Continue to blend for another 2–3 minutes, then pour into a jug and refrigerate overnight.
3 Pass through a fine sieve or strainer, and serve chilled in tall chilled glasses.

Home-made lemon liqueur

Limoncello

This delicious drink is so wickedly refreshing after a large meal. It is best kept in the freezer and poured into frosted glasses – it is the essence of lemon in a glass! It is made wherever lemons are grown. I serve this to our new guests on the first night after dinner, just to break any ice remaining after enjoying copious amounts of Sicilian food and wines! Depending on where it comes from, it is known as Lemonello, Lemoncello, Limonello or Limoncello!

MAKES ABOUT 450ML/16FL OZ/ 2 CUPS

2 large unwaxed lemons
450ml/16fl oz/2 cups pure grain alcohol
  or *grappa*
375g/13oz/1½ cups sugar

1 Scrub the lemons in warm soapy water. Rinse and dry. Pare the rind (zest) from them in long strips and place in a large preserving jar. Pour over the alcohol, seal tightly and leave in a dark place for 2 months.
2 After 2 months, put the sugar in a saucepan with 250ml/8fl oz/1 cup water and the strained juice of 1 lemon. Heat gently until the sugar is dissolved. Cool.

3 Open the preserving jar and pour in the sugar syrup. Stir well and allow to stand for a couple of hours. Stain through a fine sieve or coffee filter paper and pour into sterilized bottles. Seal and leave in a cool dark place for another week.
4 Chill or 'freeze' before serving!

Walnut liqueur

Nocino

Funnily enough, my mother makes this in our house in the south-west of France when our walnuts are still soft and green. The Italian and French recipes are the same. It must be made on the 24 June which is the Feast of St John – this is the best time! Nut liqueurs are made in much the same way all over Italy and Europe, and Franco Taruschio talks about one from Le Marche in his book Leaves from the Walnut Tree. *It is fantastic drunk on a cold winter's afternoon in front of the fire! The walnuts must still be soft enough to stick a needle right through them.*

MAKES ABOUT 1½ LITRES/2¾ PINTS/6¾ CUPS

30 green walnuts
250g/9oz/1¼ cups sugar
1 litre/1¾ pints/4 cups *grappa* or other
  pure spirit
a few strips of lemon rind (zest)
1 cinnamon stick
1 vanilla pod, split
4 cloves
a little grated nutmeg

1 Make a cross in each walnut with a sharp knife (wear rubber gloves or you will get black hands!) and place them in a large glass preserving jar with all the other ingredients. Put on the lid and shake well to mix.

2 The jar must now be left in the sunniest place for 40 days! Move around to keep it in the sun – it must 'cook'. It will look awful, but don't be discouraged!
3 Strain and filter the liquid and pour into sterilized bottles. Store in a cool dark place for about 4 months to mature.

Pine nut brittle

Pinocatte

A speciality from Perugia, where it is sold wrapped in pretty coloured paper at Christmas time. I've seen this in many markets, set in great slabs on battered trays, waiting to be broken up and weighed. As pine nuts are cheaper in Italy, I bring home masses and store them in the freezer to prevent them going rancid. I always wondered why they were so expensive, until my friend (and the photographer of this book) Gus told me that when he was a boy visiting his summer home on Elba, the lady next door would pay him and his brother to collect pine kernels and crack them open for her! They are so delicate that each kernel has to be cracked open by hand. There is a version using sesame seeds too. Very good, very sweet, very easy!

MAKES ABOUT 900G/2LBS

500g/1lb 2oz/2 cups granulated sugar
120ml/4fl oz/½ cup water
300g/11oz/2⅓ cups pine nuts

1 This is easy, but you must be ready for action as caramel burns quickly. Lightly oil two flat baking trays (sheets) or a marble surface.

2 Put the sugar in a heavy saucepan and moisten with the water. Place over a gentle heat to melt but not boil. Leave alone for 10 minutes then gently stir. Once all the sugar has melted, bring to a rapid boil and boil furiously until the syrup turns to a rich caramel colour. Immediately throw in the pine nuts and stir to coat. If it starts to set, place over a gentle heat to re-melt.

3 Immediately pour on to the oiled surface and spread out with an oiled palette knife or even an oiled lemon. Mark into desired shapes and leave to set, then break up and wrap in pretty papers.

Quince paste (candy)

Cotognata

I've seen this paste (candy) sitting in its saucer on a chair, drying in the sun on the quayside in Siracusa in early Autumn. At first I wondered what it could be, and then it dawned on me that it was cotognata. You can still find little glazed terracotta moulds in antique shops for making it – they are often mistaken for ashtrays! They always have a little impression in the bottom that will reveal itself when you turn it out. Artisan potters still make them by hand. Serve this in cubes with coffee.

MAKES ABOUT 2KG/4½ LBS

900g/2lbs ripe quinces
1 lemon, sliced thinly
sugar (see method)

1 Peel, quarter and remove the cores from the quinces. Put them in a large pan with the lemon slices. Add a little water, bring to the boil and simmer for about 45 minutes until completely soft.

2 Cool slightly then purée in a food mill or food processor. Weigh the purée and return it to the rinsed-out pan with an equal amount of sugar. Stir well and cook over a gentle heat to dissolve the sugar.

3 Bring to the boil and boil for about 1 hour – watching all the time in case it should burn, stirring occasionally. When it begins to form a paste and leave the sides of the pan, spread onto lightly oiled saucers or moulds. Cool then leave in an airy place for a few days to dry. Turn out of the mould to dry the top, then wrap in waxed paper and keep in a cool place until ready to eat.

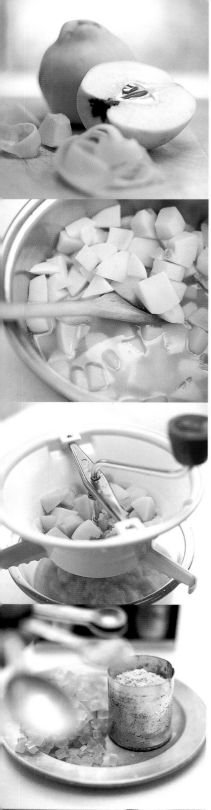

Quince and mustard preserve

Mostarda di Venezia

ANNA DEL CONTE has contributed this recipe for a *mostarda* that is rarely seen outside Italy. It is a perfect accompaniment to hot and cold meats and game dishes. Quince is a very popular fruit and is preserved in many ways throughout Italy.

MAKES 6 X 450G/1LB JARS

1.8kg/4lb quinces
1 bottle of dry white wine (750ml/
  26fl oz/3¼ cups)
grated rind (zest) and juice of
  1 unwaxed lemon
granulated sugar (see method)
5 tablespoons dried mustard powder
salt
150g/5oz candied peel, cut into small
  cubes (see recipe if you are making it)

There are two similar recipes for this Venetian preserve. Mostarda di cremona is a sweet-and-sour condiment of candied fruits with mustard sauce, a more common version of mostarda di Venezia. However, I have never met anyone in Italy who makes their own and it is difficult to make at home. My recipe here, then, Mostarda di Venezia is very easy. It is based on the recipe published in The Compleat Mustard, *a book by Robin Weir and Rosamond Man, and on a recipe given to me by my good and generous friend Maria Deana. Maria is the daughter of the famous Arturo Deana, the original owner of the Ristorante La Colomba in Venice. At La Colomba, the mostarda di Venezia was served with a sweetened mascarpone cream laced with a small glass of rum. The little pastry biscuits to accompany this delightful ensemble were shaped like a* colomba *(dove). Maria said to me, 'In this way, cheese, pudding and fruit were all supplied in a single dish.' Try it, it's a winner! ADC*

1 Peel and core the quinces and cut into pieces. Put them in a pan and cover them with the wine. Add the lemon rind (zest) and juice. Cook until soft, about 40 minutes.

2 Purée the mixture, weigh and then add the same weight in sugar. Return to the pan.

3 Dissolve the mustard powder in a little hot water and add to the purée with 1 teaspoon of salt and the candied peel. Cook gently until the liquid is reduced and the *mostarda* becomes dense, about 20–30 minutes.

4 Sterilize some jars and fill with the *mostarda*. When it is cool, cover, seal and store. Keep for about 1 month before you use it.

TIP: Buy proper candied peel sold in large segments and not the chopped up kind (or make your own!). If you cannot find quinces, try using pears instead.

Index

The master chefs

FROM THE UK
Anna del Conte
Born and educated in Milan, Anna now resides in Britain and is an award-winning food writer and food consultant with prestigious food writing awards. Her many books include *The Food of Northern Italy* and *The Gastronomy of Italy* (Pavilion).

Mary Contini
Mary is a food writer, demonstrator and one of the proprietors of the famous award-winning Italian delicatessen and wine merchant, Valvona & Crolla in Edinburgh, Scotland. Visit www.valvonacrolla.co.uk.

Ursula Ferrigno
Ursula is one of Britain's most exuberant exponents of Italian cooking. She has written several books and has contributed to various publications. She teaches cooking in La Cucina Italiana Cookery School in Umbria, Italy and demonstrates in Books for Cooks in London and appears on radio and television.

Valentina Harris
Valentina is a prolific cookery writer, teacher and food consultant who regularly broadcasts on television and radio world-wide. She has returned to live in Italy to run cookery classes at her new school in Liguria. Visit www.villavalentina.com.

Alastair Little
The innovative and exciting chef/patron of the Alastair Little restaurants in London, England and director of Tasting Places Italian Cookery Holidays where he teaches, Alastair has appeared on television and written many books. Visit www.tastingplaces.com.

Alvaro Maccione
Alvaro is the chef/patron of the famous La Famiglia, a Tuscan restaurant in London. He is also an Italian food consultant and gifted teacher. His Tuscan cookery book is called *Mamma Toscana* (Pavilion).

Claudio Pecorari
Born in Trieste, Italy, Claudio led the explosion of modern Italian cuisine with his ground-breaking Cibo, where he banned spaghetti, replacing it with gnocchi. This was followed by the fish restaurant, L'Altro. Several restaurants later, he is now an Italian food consultant and gifted teacher.

Claudia Roden
Claudia Roden is one of Britain's most acclaimed food and cookery writers. Her book, *The Food of Italy* (Pavilion), won many prestigious awards. She broadcasts on both radio and television.

Franco Taruschio
Franco has been the owner/proprietor of the Walnut Tree Inn, Abergavenny, Wales since 1963 where he has shown his vast knowledge of cooking fish, game and wild mushrooms. Now retired from the restaurant, Franco acts as an Italian food consultant and teaches. His book, *Leaves from the Walnut Tree*, is now a classic.

Francesco Zanchetta
Francesco comes from Friuli-Venezia Giulia. He worked in many Italian restaurants such as Harry's Bar in Venice before becoming head chef at Riva in London. He has taught many cookery courses in Tuscany and the Veneto.

Giuseppe Sylvestri
Giuseppe is a native of the lovely island of Capri where his family still has a restaurant. He has cooked all over the world, now busily working at Harrods, London as the Italian consultant/executive chef. He demonstrates, creates menus for special events, advises and teaches culinary gastronomic holidays all over Italy. Visit www.slowfood.com.

FROM ITALY
Anna Tasca Lanza
The Countess Tasca d'Almerita has devoted years of research into the culinary traditions of Sicily, which are fast disappearing. She runs a cooking school called The World of Regaleali at her family's country estate. Anna has also written various books.

Fulvia Sesani
Fulvia was born in Venice, and is a culinary professional who teaches and hosts cookery classes in her family's ancestral palazzo, The Palazzo Morosini della Trezza, in Venice. She is a prolific writer for worldwide magazine titles and has appeared on television.

Carla Tomasi
Carla, born in Rome, trained as a chef in London and was chef/patron at Frith's in Soho and The Peasant in Clerkenwell. Now back in Rome, she acts as a food consultant specialising in baking, and teaches cookery classes all over Italy (and Europe!).

Judy Witts Francini
Judy moved from the US to Florence in 1984 and started her cookery school La Divina Cucina in 1988, which she still runs. Visit www.divinacucina.com.

FROM THE US
Giuliano Bugialli
In 1972 Giuliano started Cooking in Florence, the first cookery school in Italy to teach in English, and it has gone from strength to strength. Giuliano also teaches abroad and on television. He has written several seminal books on Italian food and cooking, including Giuliano Bugialli's *Foods of Italy* (Stewart, Tabori and Chang). Visit www.bugialli.com.

Pino Luongo
Pino grew up in Tuscany and has lived in the US for 20 years. A highly acclaimed chef and restaurateur, he has 10 restaurants throughout the States and owns Manhattan's market, Tuscan Square. He has written books including *Simply Tuscan* (Pavilion).

Viana La Place
A second generation Italian-American and trained chef, Viana is a prolific writer and has written many books. She lives in San Francisco and spends part of each year in Italy rejuvenating and researching!

Francesca Romina
Francesca, a second generation Sicilian-New Yorker, is a skilled cook and cookery teacher who has published her own book. She regularly teaches and opened New York's Little Italy Cooking School.

FROM AUSTRALIA
Stephanie Alexander
Stephanie ran the acclaimed and award-winning Stephanie's Restaurant, then the Richmond Hill Café and Larder in Melbourne, Australia. She is a regular contributor to food publications as well as being a best selling cookery author herself. She teamed up with fellow restaurateur Maggie Beer to run cookery classes in Tuscany, and together, they wrote a book recording their memories and recipes.

Maggie Beer
An Australian restaurateur, author and food writer, Maggie began her working life farming pheasants and then opened a restaurant and started an export kitchen supplying quality foodstuffs. She is passionate about the food of Italy – especially Tuscany.